Meir Ben-Hur

CONCEPT-RICH
Mathematics
Instruction

Building a Strong Foundation for Reasoning and Problem Solving

Association for Supervision and Curriculum Development
Alexandria, Virginia USA

Association for Supervision and Curriculum Development
1703 N. Beauregard St. • Alexandria, VA 22311-1714 USA
Phone: 800-933-2723 or 703-578-9600 • Fax: 703-575-5400
Web site: www.ascd.org • E-mail: member@ascd.org
Author guidelines: www.ascd.org/write

Gene R. Carter, *Executive Director*; Nancy Modrak, *Director of Publishing*; Julie Houtz, *Director of Book Editing & Production*; Greer Beeken, *Graphic Designer*; Vivian Coss, *Production Specialist*

PAPERBACK ISBN-13: 978-1-4166-0359-7   ASCD product #106008   s6/06
PAPERBACK ISBN-10: 1-4166-0359-X
Also available as an e-book through ebrary, netLibrary, and many online booksellers (see Books in Print for ISBNs).

Quantity discounts for the paperback edition only: 10–49 copies, 10%; 50+ copies, 15%; for 500 or more copies, call 800-933-2723, ext. 5634, or 703-575-5634. For desk copies: MEMBER@ascd.org.

Library of Congress Cataloging-in-Publication Data

Ben-Hur, Meir.
Concept-rich mathematics instruction : building a strong foundation for reasoning and problem solving / Meir Ben-Hur.
p. cm.
Includes bibliographical references.
ISBN-13: 978-1-4166-0359-7 (pbk. : alk. paper)
ISBN-10: 1-4166-0359-X (pbk. : alk. paper)
1. Mathematics—Study and teaching—Methodology. 2. Concepts. 3. Mathematical analysis. 4. Problem solving. I. Title.

QA11.2.B455 2006
507.1—dc22
2006006945

13 12 11 10 09   12 11 10 9 8 7 6 5 4 3

Concept-Rich Mathematics Instruction

Foreword v

Chapter 1: Conceptual Understanding..................... 1

Chapter 2: Concept-Rich Instruction 11

Chapter 3: Misconceptions 42

Chapter 4: Solving Problems Mathematically 71

Chapter 5: Assessment................................. 109

Afterword 129

Appendix 1: Description of Teacher Activity 131

Appendix 2: Major Mathematical Concepts
    for Grades 6–8.................................... 134

References 137

Index 145

About the Author 152

ASCD cares about Planet Earth.

This book has been printed on environmentally
friendly paper.

Foreword

If we accept the centrality of Concept-Rich Instruction as highlighted in the national standard (National Council of Teachers of Mathematics [NCTM], 1989), then it is important that we develop facility in delivering that instruction. Whether we follow the most prevalent theory and research in cognitive psychology today or examine the current research emanating from mathematics educators, we will learn that teachers must play a key role in developing students' concepts and their ability to apply these concepts.

The constructivist theory that springs from Immanuel Kant's teaching tells us that the mind is an active organ and postulates that it is the teacher's responsibility to organize experiences into concepts that determine subsequent learning. Research in the field of mathematics education indicates that the teacher indeed plays a key role in meaningful learning of concepts. Without the teacher's mediation, most students do not understand the fundamental concepts, cannot make connections among the different strands within mathematics, and cannot transfer what they know beyond very particular problem situations they practiced in the classroom. Good teaching capitalizes upon the learning of core concepts. Therefore, it is important that we examine what theory and research say about the "best practices" for helping students develop new mathematical concepts.

Teaching for conceptual understanding and not for rote memorization has been the subject of much research. We know from this research that students' experiences with mathematical concepts must be much more varied than is typically the case in most classrooms. For example, researchers have warned that conceptual understanding is a product of reflection and decontextualization, activities that teachers rarely challenge students to do in the classroom. Studies on the transfer of learning point to many common teaching practices that are lacking, even inappropriate. We must inform teachers of this research and describe effective alternatives to these practices.

The typical mathematics classroom is fraught with student misconceptions, particularly in classrooms where the pace of instruction exceeds student learning. The systematic student errors that are manifest in quizzes and homework assignments point to typical student misconceptions. The research literature confirms that these errors are indeed common and not random occurrences. Perhaps more than any other subject-matter teachers, mathematics teachers will recognize and mark these student errors. They may "correct" them, or suggest what the final correct answer should be; however, teachers seldom help students analyze these errors. Thus, errors remain among the most wasted sources of information about student misconceptions. Teachers continue to treat these errors as products of "carelessness" or "laziness." Teachers rarely treat the misconceptions that are at the root of the learning problems, and students continue to hold their misconceptions sometimes throughout their mathematics studies.

Many teachers also treat mathematical problem solving as an appendix to the curriculum and fail to consider problem solving as a rich context for developing mathematical concepts. In the past, most mathematics teachers typically treated problem solving as add-on instruction to reinforce mathematics operations and procedures. This was especially true when students were tracked by ability groups, and the perceived "low performers" were taught "easier" mathematics that were often lean in problem-solving activities. The argument of this practice was logically flawed because it was based on the false premise that there are two different "mathematics." Today, experts agree that problem solving provides an important context in which students can develop their understanding of mathematics. Over the last decade, the emphasis has indeed changed. The mathematics curriculum is now organized around problem solving, and the focus has shifted from teaching how to solve mathematics problems to teaching mathematics through problem solving. Problem solving is now formally seen as an inquiry-rich context in which teachers help students to construct mathematical ideas and processes (NCTM, 1989). This change of focus provides teachers an important opportunity to learn about and more clearly identify misconceptions and "cognitive bugs" in the errors students make. Problem solving also provides a rich context for authentic assessment of students' conceptual understanding of mathematics.

Standard testing practices evaluate the *products* of mathematics—not necessarily, and often not at all, the *processes* of mathematics, especially when students err. Therefore, in addition to criterion-referenced and norm-referenced tests, it is important that teachers use authentic assessment methods that can reveal the progress in students' mathematics thinking and problem solving with tools and methods that focus not on right answers, but on reasoning itself. The tools and methods of such assessment may include continuous in-class assessment, review of student thinking in daily work, individual interviews around a problem-solving activity, and portfolio assessment that highlights the student's thinking processes.

This book complements the growing literature that focuses on particular issues of specific grade–level mathematics (see Ben-Hur, 2004). It shares the NCTM vision of school mathematics while focusing on some of the critical issues at the core of mathematics instruction. It presents an instructional approach that is responsive to the conceptual, cognitive, and meta-cognitive functions of learning and thinking mathematically. I call this practice Concept-Rich Instruction.

I wrote this book for those who wish to improve the quality of their teaching—those who wish to promote stronger, more capable mathematical thinkers among their students. I designed it for a readership that extends beyond the teachers of mathematics in all grades to include school district mathematics supervisors; mentors, coaches, and consultants in the field of professional development; teacher leaders; and all those who are interested in the best practices of mathematics education, including those concerned with their own education in this great discipline.

Chapter 1

Conceptual Understanding

Strolling about the gardens of the Academus and the Lyceum of Athens in the sunny days of 350 BCE, dining together and arguing the propositions of their masters, Plato and Aristotle, wondering students sought to resolve the great debates over the "theory of knowledge": Is *truth* discoverable by man? How is the concept of truth that is not empirical (as in mathematics) possible? Can the faculty of reason in every man be trained to find that truth? If so, how? The debates have been resonating in the great academies ever since.

In more recent times, the debates over "theory of knowledge" (now referred to as epistemology) have heated up. Philosophers such as Immanuel Kant (1724–1804) and G. W. F. Hegel (1770–1831) established the centrality of the mind as a principle of knowledge and defined knowledge as a *stage of affirmation* of reality; John Dewey (1859–1952) explained that the function of human intelligence is indeed to ensure *adaptation*. These claims set up the stage for new arguments over the finality of the concept of truth itself: Is this concept objective or subjective? The idealistic and the realistic schools of philosophy postulated that truth is objective; but others, like Karl Marx (1818–1883) and Jean Paul Sartre (1905–1980), argued that truth is only a product of our interpretations that are determined in social and historical contexts.

Philosophers are still debating the distinction between human *consciousness* and its object, and between *scientific truth* and *common sense*, drawing into the debate psychologists and educators who are entrusted with the applied perspectives of these arguments (see Suchting, 1986).

Mathematics educators, for example, are concerned with such cases as that of Debora. Debora, a 5th grade student, had mastered the procedure of adding fractions. Her teacher asked her to explain the process in front of the class:

Teacher: *Who can come to the board and show us how to solve the following problem?* [Write on the board.]

$$\frac{1}{6} + \frac{1}{3} + \frac{1}{2} =$$

Debora: *I want . . .*

Teacher: *Please come and show us. But also explain as you proceed.*

Debora: *First I see that 6 is the least common denominator, so I write 6.*

$$\frac{. . . =}{6}$$

Now, it does not change the numerator for the first fraction, it changes the second by 2 and the third by 3.

$$\frac{1 + 2 + 3 =}{6}$$

Now, I add the numerators and the answer is 6.

$$. . . = \frac{6}{6}$$

Now, 6/6 is exactly 1.

$$. . . = 1$$

Teacher: *Very good. Now, look at this drawing and explain what you see.* [Draws.]

Debora: *It's a pie with three pieces.*

Teacher: *Tell us about the pieces.*

Debora: *Three thirds.*

Teachers: *What is the difference among the pieces?*

Debora: *This is the largest third, and here is the smallest . . .*

Sound familiar? Have you ever wondered why students often understand mathematics in a very rudimentary and prototypical way, why even rich and exciting hands-on types of active learning do not always result in "real" learning of new concepts? From the psycho-educational perspective, these are the critical questions. In other words, epistemology is valuable to the extent that it helps us find ways to enable students who come with preconceived and misconceived ideas to understand a framework of scientific and mathematical concepts.

Constructivism: A New Perspective

At the dawn of behaviorism, constructivism became the most dominant epistemology in education. The purest forms of this philosophy profess that knowledge is not passively received either through the senses or by way of communication, just as meaning is not explicitly out there for grabs. Rather, constructivists generally agree that knowledge is actively built up by a "cognizing" human who needs to adapt to what is fit and viable (von Glasersfeld, 1995). Thus, there is no dispute among constructivists over the premise that one's knowledge is in a constant state of flux because humans are subject to an ever-changing reality (Jaworski, 1994, p. 16).

Although constructivists generally regard understanding as the outcome of an active process, constructivists still argue over the nature of the process of knowing. Is knowing simply a matter of recall? Does learning new concepts reflect additive or structural cognitive changes? Is the process of knowing concepts built from the "bottom up," or can it be a "top-down" process? How does new conceptual knowledge depend on experience? How does conceptual knowledge relate to procedural knowledge? And, can teachers mediate conceptual development?

Is Learning New Concepts Simply a Mechanism of Memorization and Recall?

Science and mathematics educators have become increasingly aware that our understanding of *conceptual change* is at least as important as the analysis of the concepts themselves. In fact, a plethora of research has established that concepts are mental structures of intellectual relationships, not simply a subject matter. The research indicates that the mental structures of intellectual relationships that make up mental concepts organize human experiences and human memory (Bartsch, 1998). Therefore, conceptual changes represent *structural cognitive changes,* not simply additive changes. Based on the research in cognitive psychology, the attention of research in education has been shifting from the content (e.g., mathematical concepts) to the mental predicates, language, and preconcepts. Despite the research, many teachers continue to approach new concepts as if they were simply add-ons to their students' existing knowledge—a subject of memorization and recall. This practice may well be one of the causes of misconceptions in mathematics.

Structural Cognitive Change

The notion of structural cognitive change, or *schematic change,* was first introduced in the field of psychology (by Bartlett, who studied memory in the 1930s). It became one of the basic tenets of constructivism. Researchers in mathematics education picked up on this term and have been leaning heavily on it since the 1960s, following Skemp (1962), Minsky (1975), and Davis (1984). The generally accepted idea among researchers in the field, as stated by Skemp (1986, p. 43), is that in mathematics, "to understand something is to assimilate it into an appropriate schema." A structural cognitive change is not merely an appendage. It involves the whole network of interrelated operational and conceptual schemata. Structural changes are *pervasive, central,* and *permanent.*

The first characteristic of structural change refers to its *pervasive* nature. That is, new experiences do not have a limited effect, but cause the entire cognitive structure to rearrange itself. Vygotsky (1986, p. 167) argued,

> It was shown and proved experimentally that mental development does not coincide with the development of separate psychological functions, but rather depends on changing relations between them. The development of each function, in turn, depends upon the progress in the development of the interfunctional system.

Neuroscientists describe the pervasiveness of change by referring to the neuroplasticity of the brain. A new experience causes new connections to form among the dendrites and axons attached to the brain's cells and changes the structure of the brain. When a cognitive change is structural, the structure as a whole is affected. Mathematical thinking is viewed as a structure of a connected collection of hierarchical relations. A change in part of this structure affects its relations with the other parts and thus changes the whole (Davis & Tall, 2002, pp. 131–150).

The second characteristic of structural cognitive change is *centrality,* or the autonomous, self-regulating propensity of the change. The centrality characteristic, which undergirds the theory of evolution, is represented in Vygotsky's work on cultural and social development, Piaget's work on cognitive development, and Luria's work on the neurophysiological relationship between brain and behavior (Kozulin, Mangieri, & Block, 1994). Simply stated, when one learns something and that learning results in structural change, one is prepared to learn something more advanced in the same category. For example, when adding numbers, children use the initial "count all" strategy until they recognize that certain parts of the process are redundant. They then figure out they can omit the first part and just "count on." That strategy later gives way to recalling addition facts. As this example shows, new structures act to secure themselves as they accommodate new experiences.

The third characteristic of structural change, *permanence,* asserts that structural changes are not reversible and cannot be "forgotten" because they result from the need to accommodate novel experiences. This characteristic of structural cognitive change best explains the open-ended and continuous development of a person's cognition.

Does Knowledge Develop "Bottom Up" or "Top Down"?

If knowledge develops from the "bottom up," than educators have to replace the "top-down" curriculum with a learner-centered bottom-up pedagogy and condemn any reference to mathematics as an objective body of knowledge (see Rowlands, Graham, & Berry, 2001). Is that the case? Mathematicians are the first to counter this argument by stressing that much of mathematics is based on deductive proof, not on exploration and experimentation. Most of us would assert that our own mathematics knowledge has indeed been acquired not through our own private research, but under the (at times forceful) guidance of mathematically educated people around us. The fact that the majority of people develop a mathematical knowledge that represents almost the entire history of this discipline proves that the question is moot. Rather than approaching the problem as an input-output dichotomy of choices, it is important to examine how more constructive the solution becomes when it is focused on the process of learning.

The Difference Between Conceptual Knowledge and Procedural Knowledge

In mathematics, *conceptual knowledge* (otherwise referred to in the literature as *declarative knowledge*) involves understanding concepts and recognizing their applications in various situations. Conversely, *procedural knowledge* involves the ability to solve problems through the manipulation of mathematical skills with the help of pencil and paper, calculator, computer, and so forth (see Figure 1.1). Obviously, mathematicians invented procedures based on mathematical concepts. The National Council of Teachers of Mathematics standards require that students know the procedures and understand their conceptual base. Yet, there are two contrasting theories regarding the acquisition of these two types of knowledge. One is referred to as the conceptual-change view and the other as the empiricist view.

Without neglecting the importance of experience, the conceptual-change view defines learning as the modification of current

Figure 1.1

Declarative Knowledge Versus Procedural Knowledge

Declarative (Conceptual) Knowledge	Procedural Knowledge
• Knowledge rich in relationships and understanding. • It is a connected web of knowledge, a network in which the linking relationships are as prominent as the discrete bits of information. • Examples of concepts: square, square root, function, area, division, linear equation, derivative, polyhedron. • By definition, conceptual knowledge cannot be learned by rote. It must be learned by thoughtful, reflective mental activity. • Is it possible to have conceptual knowledge/understanding about something without procedural knowledge?	• Knowledge of formal language or symbolic representations. • Knowledge of rules, algorithms, and procedures. • Can procedures be learned by rote? • Is it possible to have procedural knowledge without conceptual knowledge?

concepts and emphasizes the role of concepts in the sense people make of their experience. This theory sheds light on what it would make sense to refer to as misconceptions, how those misconceptions develop, and what should be done to correct them. In contrast, the empiricist theory of learning emphasizes the predominant role of experience in the construction of concepts.

These theories yield three different instructional practices. Two of these practices focus on what is common between concepts and procedure, and the third underscores the difference between these types of knowledge (see Figure 1.2).

Figure 1.2

Relationship Between Conceptual Knowledge and Procedural Knowledge: From Theory to Instructional Practice

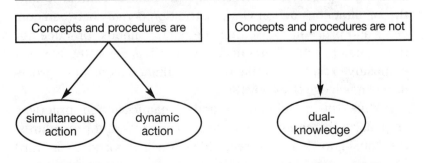

One practice considers conceptual knowledge as meta-knowledge that grows out of procedural proficiency. It is referred to as the practice of "simultaneous action" (e.g., Hiebert & Carpenter, 1992; Morris, 1999; Skemp, 1976). Instruction that follows this practice typically starts with a brief introduction of new concepts and focuses on the modeling of procedures and practice. For example, a teacher will explain why students cannot simply add the numerators of fractions with different denominators. To add such fractions they must first convert some or all of the fractions to equivalent fractions that share a common denominator. Once students do that successfully, they can add the numerators. This teacher assumes that this kind of "knowledge" about addition with fractions makes it easier for her students to learn the procedure.

The second, known as the "dynamic action practice," considers learning as a *gradual* reconceptualization that happens in the context of applying procedural knowledge to pre-existing ideas (preconceptions) (Byrnes & Wasik, 1991; Haapasalo & Kadijevich, 2000). This practice regards learning new concepts in terms of the Piagetian model of assimilation and accommodation (Nesher, 1986). Here there is no introduction of a new concept. For example, to develop the concept of numbers, children start from counting and the operation of addition. They first count all, then progress to count on, to count-on-from-larger, and to recalling addition facts—and eventually they derive new number facts from known ones. Increasingly, their number concept is featured in more compressed procedures, and their focus shifts from the procedures to the abstract idea of numbers. As with the simultaneous action view, conceptual understanding is believed to involve the procedural context. Unlike the simultaneous action view, instruction *iterates* between concepts and procedures. Neither the "simultaneous" practice nor the "dynamic action" practice, however, has consistently yielded positive results in terms of connecting conceptual to procedural knowledge (Nesher, 1986).

While the simultaneous and dynamic action practices emphasize the connection between concepts and procedures, the "dual-knowledge system" idea was proposed as a third approach, underscoring the difference between the two types of knowledge. For example, John Andersen of Carnegie Mellon University, who leads this view, argues that procedures are "housed" in task-oriented systems, and concepts reside in hierarchical structures, called schemata, that are organized by degrees of generality (Anderson, 1995). If one's procedural knowledge at all depends on her conceptual understanding—perhaps when one invents new procedures—then according to this view, learning depends on her prior conception, not on a novel conceptual understanding. In fact, Andersen argues that if there ever was an understanding of the relationship between concepts and procedures, at the end, "proceduralization" leaves aside the concepts upon which the procedural knowledge is based. This view might explain how in mathematics rote learning may be entirely divorced from conceptual understanding.

The Difference Between Direct Learning and Mediated Learning

One thing seems clear: Human cognition is not designed to discover the objective meaning of experiences, but to serve a rather more basic need—the effective organization of experiences (see the discussion of von Glasersfeld's ideas in Staver, 1998, p. 503). If students interact directly with objects or events, then their cognitive system organizes experiences by idiosyncratic frameworks, and only rarely do students feel a need to discover another framework by which to organize the experiences. When teachers mediate this interaction, however, learning follows a different course simply because the need to communicate their thoughts forces students to represent and reflect on their experiences—the need to report and answer questions verbally forces them to examine and even revise their concepts of reality (Vygotsky, 1978). The agents that mediate this learning are featured in the language and symbols of the social culture. In this way, teaching and cooperative learning can challenge a student's state of mind so much that it leads to a need to reconstruct his understanding of things.

Summary

The general view among philosophers, cognitive psychologists, and educators is that humans develop concepts through an active process of adaptation to new and different experiences. Constructivists agree that new concepts are not simply facts to be memorized and later recalled, but knowledge that reflects structural cognitive changes. As such, new concepts permanently change the way students learn, the way they think about facts they encounter, the way they process events around them, and the way they solve problems. The socioculturist view that has gained acclaim over the last two decades emphasizes the critical role of mediation in conceptual development. It underscores the idea that students need to regularly discuss and reflect on their learning with a knowledgeable teacher—and with one another—if they are to develop a solid understanding of concepts. Debates over the most effective classroom practices for the development of students' new concepts are continuing: whether instruction should be based on the idea that concepts are best built from the bottom up or from the top down—that is, whether teachers should engage students in new experiences first and then help the concepts evolve, or present a new concept and then provide students many experiences with their applications.

Chapter 2

Concept-Rich Instruction

Concept-Rich Instruction is based on the generally accepted constructivist views of effective teaching and takes a clear position on the issues that are still debated. It is founded upon two undisputed principles. One principle is that learning new concepts reflects a cognitive process. The other is that this process involves reflective thinking that is greatly facilitated through mediated learning.

The idea that learning is progressive, structural, cognitive change has been quite common among educators. For example, Bloom's *Taxonomy of Educational Objectives* described all learning as a progression through five phases: analysis, synthesis, comprehension, application, and ultimately evaluation. Mathematics education researchers have consistently based their theories upon this idea. Even the behaviorists among them—for example, Robert Gange, a leading experimental psychologist from Florida State University, who prefers to use such verbs as *state, define,* and *identify,* rather than *know* and *understand* on statements of educational objectives—explain the learning of mathematical concepts in terms of a hierarchy (Gange, 1985). Obviously, cognitive researchers have done it all along. Bruner (1991) spoke of stages in concept development that progress from enactive, to iconic, and eventually into symbolic. For Richard Skemp, world-renowned British pioneer theorist in the psychology of mathematics, the idea that there are different levels of conceptual understanding was fundamental (Skemp, 1976) and served as an important precursor to the contemporary research on cognition in mathematics (Asiala et al., 1996; Biggs & Collins, 1982; Sfard, 1992; Sfard & Linchevski, 1994; Van Hiele, 1986).

It is also an established fact that learning mathematical concepts involves reflection. Learning new concepts starts from sheer perception and isolated action (perhaps a model produced by a teacher) and ends in the independent ability of application; from an attention that might be random and unfocused on peripheral and incidental features to an awareness of what is mathematically critical; from overt action to an internalized and abstract idea (Davis & Tall, 2002; Harris, 1998; Skemp, 1976, p. 190). This reflective process is facilitated and accelerated through interaction with a teacher and with other students—or *mediated learning.*

Concept-Rich Instruction is essentially a process with five components (see Figure 2.1). As pointed out by research in mathematics education, as well as in studies on transfer of learning, each of the components is clearly defined, the components are somewhat consequential, and they are jointly necessary for helping students understand mathematics. Following are the five components of Concept-Rich Instruction:

1. **Practice.** Learning concepts requires sufficient appropriate practice.

2. **Decontextualization.** Students must experience a variety of applications to be able to generate a concept.

3. **Encapsulating a generalization in words.** Students develop conceptual understanding, or meaning, through reflection and verbalization.

4. **Recontextualization.** Students must identify new applications for concepts and use concepts to connect new experiences with past or concurrent experiences.

5. **Realization.** Teachers must encourage transfer into new experiences across the curriculum.

Figure 2.1

The Five Components of Concept-Rich Instruction

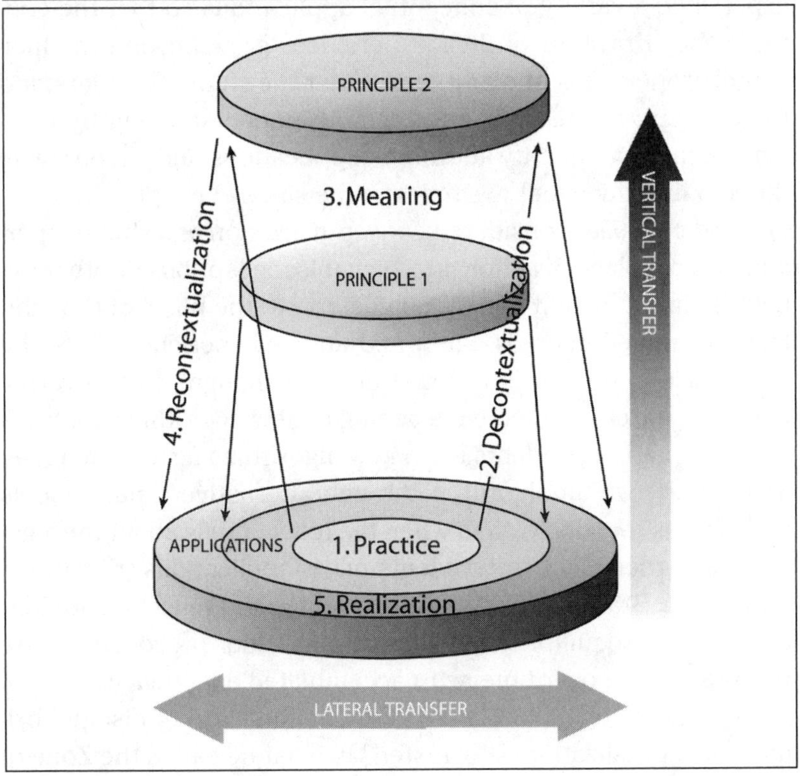

1. Practice

Direct instruction considers practice as the drill that follows the presentation and demonstration of a concept. Educators who espouse this approach have learned to present the concept, show examples, check for understanding, and then proceed to guided practice that drills students on use of the concept. With Concept-Rich Instruction, this sequence does not work well because students who lack prior knowledge of the concept receive the "telling" with deaf ears and blank stares. The concept makes no sense to these students. When it is time to practice, many are practicing without understanding what they are doing.

In the Concept-Rich approach, practice is not limited to drill. It involves novel activities that are all based on the same concept. Such practice represents not only homework, but class work as well. The teacher starts with an intriguing problem and later provides a variety of other problems. Eventually, students experience a variety of conceptual applications so that the concepts they draw out of their experiences grow beyond the incidental properties of the problems. After the students understand the concept, the teacher reinforces the understanding by challenging them to identify additional applications and encouraging them to find divergent examples of the same concept.

Piaget (1995a) considered conceptualization as a shift of operation from a plane of action, in which misconceptions or other difficulties interfere and create "confusion," to the plane of thought. First, he argued, there is a new and unique experience. Once the experience is over, it is enacted upon in thought on the verbal plane. Research on effective teaching of new algorithms confirms this observation. Students learn new algorithms faster when they first experience an algorithm through alternative visual models and discuss their logic, than when the teacher tells about the algorithm and then drills the students on its applications (Kilpatrick, Swafford, & Bradford, 2001). When practice and reflection are iterated, the disequilibria between action and preconcepts are resolved slowly over time, with accumulated experience.

Vygotsky (1978) recognized that, at the state of disequilibrium, conceptualization is "arrested" in what he called the Zone of Proximal Development. Students may say the right thing, but they fail to enact it. Likewise, they may do the right thing, but fail to explain it. Students lose "premature" concepts over time if they do not continue to practice and reflect upon them. Thus, conceptualization depends upon (1) the amount, (2) the nature, and (3) the novelty and challenge of the practice structured by the teacher.

How Much Practice Is Necessary?

Because practice consumes time, and teachers are often pressured to move on with the curriculum, the first thing they compromise is practice time. The rushed teacher may use false indicators that practice has been sufficient and believe she can safely proceed to the next level. These indicators may include her judgment that a "reasonable" number of students have already reached the mastery level. Or it may simply be that the bell signals the end of the class period and, therefore, the end of this guided practice because students must move to the next class. Worse, the rush may occur because the students have used up all of the available practice samples. In all cases when guided practice is not sufficient and, for the students who need more practice, the teacher moves on prematurely, the teacher and students inevitably will end up spending much more time in later remedial work trying to rebuild the same concepts—not only from the point in the process that was already reached, but from the beginning.

Assigned homework is unguided practice. For some students, practice without guidance does not necessarily solve the problems created by shortened teacher-guided practice. Assigned homework does not work well for all students, particularly not for low-performing students who need more time and mediation to form the concepts. Without the mediation, these students are more likely to practice poorly or to practice the wrong elements (Good & Brophy, 2000). In many cases, these students are likely not to practice at all, and these are the students who most need the practice.

The amount of practice over time must reflect the nonlinear nature of learning. New experiences require more time and effort than later experiences. The early experiences must be simple, and later ones must be progressively more complex. Students must experience new concepts repeatedly until the teacher can determine that students have indeed crystallized the concept in their minds.

Nature of Repetition

Many theories (e.g., those following Dienes, 1960) suggest that students must experience a variety of conceptual applications so that the concepts they draw out of them neglect the incidental properties. In the reality of standardized mathematics achievement tests, however, teachers are often misled into spending excessive time drilling students on specific computational "skills." Teachers prepare students for anticipated forms and types of standardized tests, and students develop rigid habits that often do not permit conceptualization. For example, teachers would have students complete several worksheets solving linear equations (ax + b = c) where the coefficients are all natural numbers. This practice is of limited value and, because it cannot possibly involve every variation of the linear equation, it leaves the students conceptually ill prepared to deal with new varieties. A student may perform well if a test asks for the specific equation forms that students practiced with; however, it is highly predictable that the same student will perform poorly if test items don't match this form. Effective practice with linear equations should gradually involve various forms, including rational positive and negative coefficients. Research indicates the advantage of experiencing variance in conceptual applications to the development of conceptual understanding (Schmidt, McKnight, & Raizen, 1997).

Novelty and Challenge

To avoid mundane and repetitive work and maintain students' reflective practice, it is important for teachers to design practice tasks of optimal challenge. To achieve a high level of student success, teachers must avoid practice tasks that are too easy as well as practice tasks that are too difficult. As Madeline Hunter, professor of educational administration and teacher education at UCLA, and the creator of the Instructional Theory Into Practice (ITIP) teaching model, used to explain in her addresses to teachers, like the violinist who wants to make beautiful music and thus tunes the strings at an optimal tension, neither too loose nor too taut, the effective teacher will fine-tune the practice tasks.

Moreover, as indicated earlier, the effective teacher will match the level of task difficulty with the students' improving abilities. While preparing or searching for tasks that are novel, the teacher will also make sure that each task is built on prior knowledge and existing cognitive abilities. Time on each task must be relative to students' progress, and the emphasis must always be on student explanations and the development of sustainable meaning. This way, practice is not laborious and tedious. As the example in Figure 2.2 indicates, there is a variety of ways for a teacher to do this.

Figure 2.2

Novelty and Change in Practice

After students have learned how to multiply multidigit numbers, the teacher may vary the practice by applying the process backwards:

$$
\begin{array}{r}
3\ \square \\
\times\ \square\ 6 \\
\hline
1\ \square\ \square \\
+\ \square\ \square\ \square \\
\hline
1\ \square\ 9\ \square
\end{array}
$$

Can you figure out the missing digits?

After students have practiced the Pythagorean theorem, they may enjoy applying it to produce the "cool" Irrational Spiral.

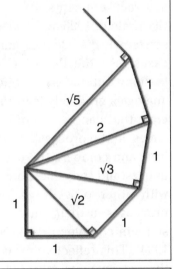

If students know the Pythagorean theorem and have learned to find the area of squares and of right triangles, the teacher may challenge them to prove the distributive rule as it applies to geometry:

Show that the area of the big square (4" by 4") is equal to the sum of its 12 sections.

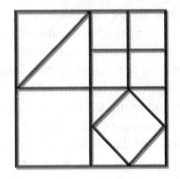

2. Decontextualization

Teachers often spend excessive amounts of instructional time on exercising and drilling procedural skills and spend very little classroom time on discussions of concepts. Research shows a need for varied, balanced attention to each. Indeed, research shows that because conceptual development is a product of metacognitive reflection that can be facilitated and accelerated through mediation, this varied and balanced attention to procedures and concepts is the single most important predictor of student achievement (Kilpatrick et al., 2001).

Experts generally agree that concepts develop through a reflective process. Concepts cannot simply be passed from one person to another by talk, because each individual must abstract concepts from his or her own experience (von Glasersfeld, 1996, p. 5). Piaget (1995b) showed that the process starts with analogies among seemingly different individual cases (see the Piagetian-based SOLO (structure of observed learning outcomes) Taxonomy in Biggs & Collins, 1982). These analogies gradually lead to an extrapolation of a common principle that can be extended over the whole universe of experiences. In the process, students gradually learn to consider, analyze, and compare the procedure without a need to perform it, understand the conditions under which it works, or combine it with other procedures. Students learn to see mathematical processes in their entirety, without the details, rather than as steps in complex procedures (Sfard, 1992; Sfard & Linchevski, 1994). This reflective process is facilitated by language—either through writing or through a classroom discourse (Asiala et al., 1996; Shepard, 1993).

The process is sometimes referred to in the research literature as decontextualization. It is the second essential component of the Concept-Rich Instruction model. Like the first component, practice, the effective teacher determines the quality of decontextualization (see Figure 2.3).

Decontextualization is stimulated by variable and sufficient practice. Such practice provides a framework and incentive for discussions that help students recognize the relationships

Figure 2.3
Three Representations of $1\frac{3}{4} : \frac{1}{2}$

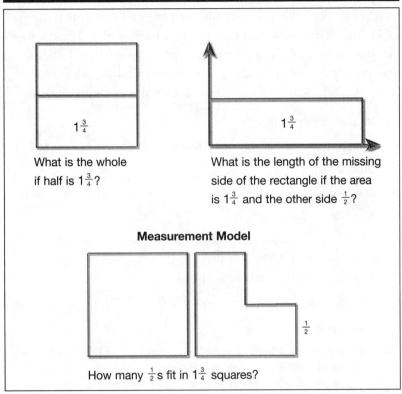

What is the whole if half is $1\frac{3}{4}$?

What is the length of the missing side of the rectangle if the area is $1\frac{3}{4}$ and the other side $\frac{1}{2}$?

Measurement Model

How many $\frac{1}{2}$s fit in $1\frac{3}{4}$ squares?

existing among the various representations of the concept in focus, and identify their core similarities. In this context, the point of classroom discourse that follows practice is to develop students' understanding, not merely to check their work.

Teachers can lead students to reflect about planning, monitoring, comparing, contrasting, classifying, summarizing, evaluating their work, and analyzing their errors. As shown in the early *Teacher Expectations and Student Achievement* research, Marzano's meta-analysis of effective classroom strategies (Marzano, Pickering, & Pollack, 2005), and other studies of effective teaching in mathematics (Kerman & Martin, 1980), this reflection is best fostered by "higher-order" questioning, wait time, encouragement of divergent responses, and analyses of student errors and inconsistencies.

Higher-Order Questioning

To prove that concepts and skills can themselves be acquired neither empirically nor through teaching, but rather through recollection, Socrates attempted to demonstrate that Meno's uneducated slave had enough knowledge to invent by himself the Pythagorean theorem (a square whose area is twice that of a given square is the square on its diagonal; see Figure 2.4).

Meno, the dialogue in Plato

Soc. Tell me, boy, do you know that a figure like this is a square?

Boy. I do.

Soc. And you know that a square figure has these four lines equal?

Boy. Certainly.

Soc. And these lines which I have drawn through the middle of the square are also equal?

Boy. Yes.

Soc. A square may be of any size?

Boy. Certainly.

Soc. And if one side of the figure be of two feet, and the other side be of two feet, how much will the whole be? Let me explain: if in one direction the space was of two feet, and in other direction of one foot, the whole would be of two feet taken once?

Boy. Yes.

Soc. But since this side is also of two feet, there are twice two feet?

Boy. There are.

Soc. Then the square is of twice two feet?

Boy. Yes.

Soc. And how many are twice two feet? Count and tell me.

Boy. Four, Socrates.

Soc. And might there not be another square twice as large as this, and having like this the lines equal?

Boy. Yes.

Soc. And of how many feet will that be?

Boy. Of eight feet.

Figure 2.4

Socratic Questioning

In Plato's dialogue, Meno leads a slave boy to a discovery that the area of the large square is twice the area of the smaller one. There is a discussion of the nature of the knowledge and origin of such facts.

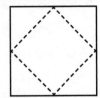

Soc. And now try and tell me the length of the line which forms the side of that double square: this is two feet—what will that be?

Boy. Clearly, Socrates, it will be double.

Soc. Do you observe, Meno, that I am not teaching the boy anything, but only asking him questions; and now he fancies that he knows how long a line is necessary in order to produce a figure of eight square feet; does he not?

Men. Yes.

Soc. And does he really know?

Men. Certainly not.

Soc. He only guesses that because the square is double, the line is double.

Men. True.

Soc. Observe him while he recalls the steps in regular order. (To the Boy.) Tell me, boy, do you assert that a double space comes from a double line? Remember that I am not speaking of an oblong, but of a figure equal every way, and twice the size of this—that is to say of eight feet; and I want to know whether you still say that a double square comes from double line?

Boy. Yes.

Soc. But does not this line become doubled if we add another such line here?

Boy. Certainly.

Soc. And four such lines will make a space containing eight feet?

Boy. Yes.

Soc. Let us describe such a figure: Would you not say that this is the figure of eight feet?

Boy. Yes.

Soc. And are there not these four divisions in the figure, each of which is equal to the figure of four feet?

Boy. True.

Soc. And is not that four times four?

Boy. Certainly.

Soc. And four times is not double?

Boy. No, indeed.

Soc. But how much?

Boy. Four times as much.

Soc. Therefore the double line, boy, has given a space, not twice, but four times as much.

Boy. True.

Soc. Four times four are sixteen—are they not?

Boy. Yes.

Soc. What line would give you a space of eight feet, as this gives one of sixteen feet—do you see?

Boy. Yes.

Soc. And the space of four feet is made from this half line?

Boy. Yes.

Soc. Good; and is not a space of eight feet twice the size of this, and half the size of the other?

Boy. Certainly.

Soc. Such a space, then, will be made out of a line greater than this one, and less than that one?

Boy. Yes; I think so.

Soc. Very good; I like to hear you say what you think. And now tell me, is not this a line of two feet and that of four?

Boy. Yes.

Soc. Then the line which forms the side of eight feet ought to be more than this line of two feet, and less than the other of four feet?

Boy. It ought.

Soc. Try and see if you can tell me how much it will be.

Boy. Three feet.

Soc. Then if we add a half to this line of two, that will be the line of three. Here are two and there is one; and on the other side, here are two also and there is one: and that makes the figure of which you speak?

Boy. Yes.

Soc. But if there are three feet this way and three feet that way, the whole space will be three times three feet?

Boy. That is evident.

Soc. And how much are three times three feet?

Boy. Nine.

Soc. And how much is the double of four?

Boy. Eight.

Soc. Then the figure of eight is not made out of a line of three?

Boy. No.

Soc. But from what line? Tell me exactly; and if you would rather not reckon, try and show me the line.

Boy. Indeed, Socrates, I do not know.

Soc. Do you see, Meno, what advances he has made in his power of recollection? He did not know at first, and he does not know now, what is the side of a figure of eight feet: but then he thought that he knew, and answered confidently as if he knew, and had no difficulty; now he has a difficulty, and neither knows nor fancies that he knows.

Men. True.

Soc. Is he not better off in knowing his ignorance?

Men. I think that he is.

Soc. If we have made him doubt, and given him the "torpedo's shock," have we done him any harm?

Men. I think not.

Soc. We have certainly, as would seem, assisted him in some degree to the discovery of the truth; and now he will wish to remedy his ignorance, but then he would have been ready to tell all the world again and again that the double space should have a double side.

Men. True.

Soc. But do you suppose that he would ever have inquired into or learned what he fancied that he knew, though he was really ignorant of it, until he had fallen into perplexity under the idea that he did not know, and had desired to know?

Men. I think not, Socrates.

Soc. Then he was the better for the torpedo's shock?

Men. I think so.

Soc. Mark now the further development. I shall only ask him, and not teach him, and he shall share the inquiry with me: and do you watch and see if you find me telling or explaining anything to him, instead of eliciting his opinion. Tell me, boy, is not this a square of four feet which I have drawn?

Boy. Yes.

Soc. And now I add another square equal to the former one?

Boy. Yes.

Soc. And a third, which is equal to either of them?

Boy. Yes.

Soc. Suppose that we fill up the vacant corner?

Boy. Very good.

Soc. Here, then, there are four equal spaces?

Boy. Yes.

Soc. And how many times larger is this space than this other?

Boy. Four times.

Soc. But it ought to have been twice only, as you will remember.

Boy. True.

Soc. And does not this line, reaching from corner to corner, bisect each of these spaces?

Boy. Yes.

Soc. And are there not here four equal lines which contain this space?

Boy. There are.

Soc. Look and see how much this space is.

Boy. I do not understand.

Soc. Has not each interior line cut off half of the four spaces?

Boy. Yes.

Soc. And how many spaces are there in this section?

Boy. Four.

Soc. And how many in this?

Boy. Two.

Soc. And four is how many times two?

Boy. Twice.

Soc. And this space is of how many feet?

Boy. Of eight feet.

Soc. And from what line do you get this figure?

Boy. From this.

Soc. That is, from the line which extends from corner to corner of the figure of four feet?

Boy. Yes.

Soc. And that is the line which the learned call the diagonal. And if this is the proper name, then you, Meno's slave, are prepared to affirm that the double space is the square of the diagonal?

Boy. Certainly, Socrates.

Soc. What do you say of him, Meno? Were not all these answers given out of his own head?

Men. Yes, they were all his own. (Plato, trans. 1892)

In Plato's *Meno,* the false assumption is that during the discourse with the slave, Socrates did not engage in any form of teaching. In fact, the discourse modeled great teaching. Socrates used leading questions to get the slave to notice the diagonal by explicitly bringing it up himself; his questions engaged the slave in reasoning—that is, deducing the (not previously noticed) consequences of his prior misconceptions; and the questioning progressed logically from the initial preconceptions to the Pythagorean generalization. Over the centuries this form of teaching became known as "Socratic questioning."

As Plato's *Meno* demonstrates, teacher questioning can be an effective instructional tool. Questions that involve comparing experiences, grouping them, generalizing common ideas from such comparisons, and anticipating future experiences based on such generalizations make the decontextualization possible. Such questions may not be raised in the learners' minds without the teacher's mediation. It is teachers who ask students to look back when they are looking forward, to anticipate when they are fixated with a past or present experience, to compare an individual experience with other experiences when they may be content with an episode, and to look into the experiences of their classmates when they are complacent with their own. It is teachers who ask students to label their experiences and define their learning processes and outcomes when the students could otherwise act without reflection. Because they have already done their assignment, students conclude that they are ready for the next. This type of teaching describes an extensive journey that many teachers appreciate but that few travel on a daily basis (Marzano et al., 2005).

Marzano and his colleagues distinguish between two types of higher-order questions: questions that facilitate analyses and questions that elicit inferences (see Figure 2.5).

Both analysis and inference are necessary for decontextualization. Asking students to analyze their experience leads them to recognize the problems with their preconceived notions, the novelty of the experience, or the reason for an error. This kind of

Figure 2.5
Higher-Order Questions

Analysis Questions	Inference Questions
• Call for arguments that support or reject given positions	• Facilitate the process of "filling in" missing information
• Call for different perspectives, processes, or solutions	
• Examine errors	

analysis will establish a cognitive disequilibrium that the student needs to have resolved. Simply put, it will expose the student to what he does not know.

Asking students to infer elevates their thinking beyond the evidence, extending their experience toward a generalization. Inference questions not only mediate the decontextualization of meaning, but also facilitate a reflective classroom discourse.

Wait Time

Yet another feature of reflective classroom discourses is teacher wait time. Mary Budd Rowe's seminal wait time research showed that low-achieving students do not have enough time in the classroom to reflect and respond to teachers' questions thoughtfully (Rowe, 1996). Her research also showed that those students are more likely than high-achieving peers to be given the answers rather then being challenged by a teacher's questions. Wait time is a familiar and common issue of discussions among teachers. The mounting pressure on teachers to cover more content in a set amount of time makes it difficult for teachers to practice wait time in the classroom. Wait time is essential for students to reflect upon questions that are relevant to their conception of new mathematical ideas, and probing is exactly the help these students need if they cannot reach the correct answer at once. Teachers must wait longer and listen carefully to students' responses so teachers can intervene by asking probing questions where necessary. In the long run, wait time saves remedial work and enhances the learning environment.

Encouragement of Divergent Responses

Research on best practices identifies efficient classrooms as those that function as a community of learners in which ideas expressed by different students warrant respect and response and have the potential to stimulate learning (Ball & Bass, 2000). Students must recognize that many strategies may work in solving a problem and that authority for what is correct or not lies in the logic and structure of mathematics, not in the status of the teacher or a student. Effective teachers promote divergent responses and involve all their students as equal members of a learning community.

Student Reflection over Errors

To promote learning, teachers must understand how students make errors and treat errors with great care. The next chapter analyzes types of student errors by their different causes. In terms of decontextualization, however, it is important to acknowledge that errors provide important substance for classroom discourse and questioning. The function of classroom discussion of errors is to reveal to students where they have only a tenuous grasp of a new concept. Unfortunately, research shows that student errors are rarely considered as instructional tools (Kilpatrick et al., 2001). The examples in Figures 2.6 and 2.7 are common.

It is clear that although Linda has mastered the numerical operations with fractions, she still fails to understand their meaning.

It is essential for student learning that teachers encourage students to evaluate and explain their mathematical thinking, to compare their work with other students' work, and to identify and explain the differences and the processes that produced them. When a misconception is evident, the teacher must guide the students' consideration of the error, analyze and assert the "off thinking," and encourage students to assist each other in correcting the misconception. In many cases, the effective teacher will call upon past experience and predict the occurrence of a misconception. In addition to building into the lesson plan the appropriate time to deal with predictable misconceptions, effective teachers must be

Figure 2.6

An Example of Students' False Perception of Mathematical Knowledge

Linda, a 6th grade student, could compute. Her math grade indicated that she was a good student.

$$\frac{1}{2} + \frac{1}{3} + \frac{1}{6} = \frac{6}{6} = 1$$
$$\frac{6}{6} = 1$$

However, when asked to explain the following chart, she named the largest piece of the pie as the "largest third" and the smallest piece as the "smallest third."

Figure 2.7
Misconceptions in Geometry

Middle school students use irrelevant attributes in their classification in geometry. Examples can be found in students' misconceptions of right angles, isosceles triangles, the height of a triangle, and more. Students who experience such misconceptions do not decontextualize the concepts from the "vertical-horizontal" page sides that constitute their frames of reference.

For example, although students easily identify (e) as a right triangle, many have difficulties recognizing (f) as such, and (g) is even more difficult for them to recognize. Similarly, they recognize (b) as an isosceles triangle, but have difficulties recognizing (c) as such, and even more so (e).

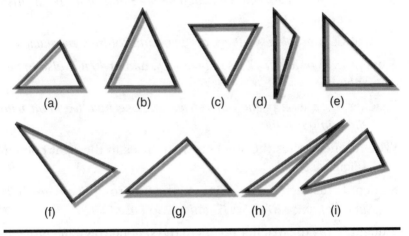

flexible and deviate from lesson plans when students encounter unanticipated difficulties or raise interesting questions.

Consider the following discussion in a 6th grade classroom:

Teacher: *Let's look at homework problems 46 and 47, on page 173* (the University of Chicago Math Project).

The problems:

Problem 46: In March 1993, one Israeli shekel was worth 37¢. So a blouse that cost 80 shekels was worth about how many dollars?

Problem 47: In March 1993, one Irish punt was worth about $1.49. If a shillelagh sold for 2.98 punts, how much was that in U.S. dollars?

[Two students present solutions to one of the problems by writing them on the board. After a short discussion in which an error in one student's work is corrected with the help of the class, the lesson continues.]

Teacher: *Now, are these two problems the same?*

Student A: *No.*

Teacher: *Let's find the difference between the two problems.*

[Teacher draws a table with two columns and writes the following responses in the left column.]

Student A: *In problem 46 it's in cents; in 47 it's in dollars.*

Student B: *In problem 46 it's Israeli shekel, and in 47 it's in Irish punt and shillelagh.*

Student C: *In problem 47 there are two kinds of Irish currencies.*

Student D: *In problem 47 it's only money, and in 46 it is also to buy a blouse.*

Teacher: *Let's look at the differences and see how we dealt with them in our solution.*

[The teacher writes the students' responses in the right column (Figure 2.8).]

Student F: [as the teacher points to the first row] *There are 100¢ in a dollar, so 37¢ is 0.37 dollars. So I used $0.37.*

Student D: [as the teacher points to the second row] *The problem is how many shill . . . not punts, so I had to answer the question.*

Teacher: *How did you figure out that you have to find how many shillelaghs?*

Figure 2.8
Organization of Students' Responses on the Board

Problem 46 is in cents and Problem 47 is in dollars	use $0.37 instead of 37¢
Problem 46 has one Israeli currency Problem 47 has two Irish currencies	decide which currency we need to report
Problem 47 has two kinds of Irish currencies	figure 2.98 shillelagh for every 1 punt
Problem 47 includes only money Problem 46 includes money to buy a blouse	figure the value of 80 shekels in dollars

Student G: [reads the problem] *If a shillelagh sold for 2.98 punts, how much was that in U.S. dollars?*

Teacher: *So, what is the word "that" referring to?*

Student B: *Shill* . . . [Teacher completes the second row in the table, and points to the fourth row.]

Student J: *A blouse is like the other currency.*

Teacher: *How is it possible?*

Student J: *It is worth 80 shekels.*

Student D: *So everything is like money* . . .

Student A: *Everything is worth money, so everything is like money* . . .

Student D: *Not everything is worth money. The sun is not worth* . . .

Teacher [interrupting]: *Boys and girls, the problem is not if everything is worth money, but if a price of something can be converted from one currency to another.*

Student D: *Yes.*

Teacher: *Then* . . . [writes in the table] *figure the value of 80 shekels in dollars.*

Teacher: *Now, look at the table and tell me what is common to both problems?*

Student C: *They are about money ex* . . .

Student F: *Exchange. Like when you go to the bank when you travel* . . .

Teacher: *True, it's when we change units of currency.*

Teacher: *And what do we do when we change from one currency to another?*

Student F: *We multiply what one unit is worth by how many units of the other.*

In this case, as is generally true, decontextualization does not automatically result in the development of deep meaning. It takes time and guidance. Without one or the other, the students may move on with some "getting it" and many others not. So, how exactly does meaning develop?

3. Meaning: Encapsulating a Generalization in Words

Students must learn to define concepts and elaborate upon them in their general form. They must learn to encapsulate their conceptual understanding in words and symbols. The cognitive process that involves encapsulation in words and symbols of a new meaning that is derived from a multitude of experiences, comparison, and decontextualization is complex and requires careful teacher mediation. It involves accommodation of the new concept in the hierarchy of concepts (see Figure 2.9).

Independent learning does not necessarily result in conceptualization. Encapsulating a generalization in words involves the complete restructuring of the cognitive schema (Shepard, 1993).

Piaget recognized that children do not necessarily abstract a law that governs analogous cases. Instead, they may "synchronically compromise" seemingly conflicting forms of action. For example, he describes 7-year-old children who reasoned "boats float because they are light. But big boats float because they are heavy" (Piaget, 1995b, p. 110). This is true to different degrees with adults as well. It took humanity "a Newton" (and an apple) to discover the law of gravity that was overlooked by his contemporary fellow scientists and all their predecessors. Inevitably, a novice shall struggle to find the meanings of his craft that his expert fellow knows so well.

Meaning guides thinking. Meaningless action can only reproduce, copy, or imitate other actions. It does not result in transfer to other than identical situations. The meaningless repetition, copying, and imitation that are typical in mindless practice (and lack of thinking) render students unable to know what to do with standardized test items that fall outside those drills practiced. Meaningful learning results in conceptualization.

Figure 2.9

Conceptualization and Deep Meaning

Ask a teacher why she consistently teaches in a particular way, and you will hear what she means by teaching.	Ask a chess player why he made a particular move, and he will consistently show you that a move is guided by a meaningful concept.

Concepts transcend their particular applications. Eventually, concepts do not even disclose the specific content or context from which they were induced. For example, after several learning experiences, Linda should understand that all 1/a's always represent equal parts of the same whole. This idea does not disclose the nature of the tasks from which it originated—whether Linda learned it from dividing a pizza pie, a set of candies, a given quantity of liquid, or otherwise. When she knows this concept, she is ready to apply it to a wide variety of other situations. How does Linda know that all 1/a's always represent equal parts of the same whole, even though she experienced this fact only with limited applications?

Many teachers think that teaching concepts means "telling" about them. Conversely, others argue that students independently construct mathematics concepts from their own experiences. Research supports neither of these views. It shows that conceptualization is not simply an exercise in memory, and it also shows that the alternative theory of "discovery learning" does not work for many, particularly lower-achieving, students (Piaget, 1995b). Discovery alone certainly cannot produce all the logic that students must recognize in mathematics, and experiences cannot grasp the infinite. Students need guidance in forming new mathematics concepts and help in correcting their misconceptions.

Research shows that if all teachers do is ask open-ended questions, respect students' ideas, accept them, and encourage students to think, then they are likely to be greatly disappointed about their students' learning of new mathematics concepts. Research also shows that telling the concept does little to correct misconceptions. It is necessary for teachers to guide students' reasoning toward the accepted scientific view through careful "scaffolding." Teachers must intervene by asking guiding questions, correcting, and engaging students with self-evaluation and reflection.

Consider the way the discussion in a 6th grade mathematics classroom (the earlier part of which is presented on pages 29–31) reached a conceptual understanding:

Teacher: *Now, look at the table and tell me what is common to both problems?*

Student C: *They are about money ex . . .*

Student F: *Exchange. Like when you go to the bank when you travel . . .*

Teacher: *True, it's when we change units of currency.*

Teacher: *And what do we do when we change from one currency to another?*

Student F: *We multiply what one unit is worth by how many units of the other.*

Teacher: *What have we learned here as a principle that is always true?*

Student D: *When we change currencies, we have to know what one unit in one currency is worth in the other currency—then we multiply it to know what a number of units is worth.*

Teacher: [writes Student D's response on the board] *Is this principle only true for the exchange of currencies?*

Student A: *No, it is also when we learned about units of measurements, like inches and centimeters.*

Teacher: *So, let us change the word currency in our principle to say "units."*

[Writes on the board:]

> *Whenever we change quantities in one unit to another unit, we use what we know about the worth of one unit and multiply it by the rate of exchange to know the quantity in terms of the other unit.*

The conclusion reached in this lesson represents an important concept of measurement. Figure 2.10 provides other examples of concepts that students must develop in middle school.

Two problems have been identified in the construction of new concepts (von Glasersfeld, 1996, p. 5). First, the conceptual structures may differ among individual students, and the meaning that students build up for themselves may likewise differ from one student to another. Second, teachers must not assume that meaning is transported from a speaker to a listener as if the language is fixed somewhere outside its users. To avoid these problems, teachers must listen carefully as their students define and explain their generalizations and observe the students' work as they apply their new understanding to additional and different applications.

Figure 2.10

Examples of Middle School Mathematical Concepts

- Parts and wholes are relative terms.
- Ratio is the relation between numbers, not the numbers themselves.
- Percents comprise a subset of decimals that comprise a subset of universal fractions ($\frac{a}{b}$).
- We can only add and subtract like terms (objects of the same category, same units of measurements, common denomination, same algebraic notations).
- The distributive, associative, and commutative rules apply to all additions and multiplications of rational numbers.

When it appears that students have grasped a new concept, the teacher must direct them to apply the new concept consistently to new situations. New applications shape and reinforce the new concepts. Adding variations to the concept helps the learner to reach a greater generalization of the concept and to embrace a wider set of possible applications. Compare, for example, the evolution of children's notion of Earth's shape and the direction of "down" on the flat earth to the "absolute down" on the spherical earth and the concept of gravity. This deeper understanding of Earth and gravity reflects a conceptual movement to a deeper, more generalized concept (Baxter, 1989; Nussbaum, 1985). (See Figure 2.11.)

Figure 2.11

The Evolution of Children's Notion of Earth's Shape

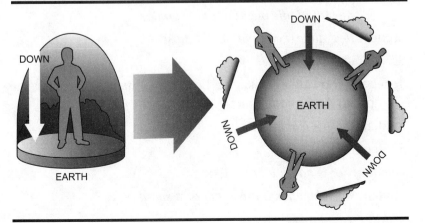

4. Recontextualization

Many educators often assume that a new concept automatically provides the higher level from which students will successfully deal with all future applications and recategorize relevant past experiences. As research indicates otherwise, experts argue that conceptualization is complete only when the learner is able to recontextualize it in new and untried experiences (Shepard, 1993). New concepts do not get automatically transferred, and recontextualizing new concepts must be coached.

Recontextualization refers to the application of new concepts to past or current experiences that are contextually different from experiences that constituted their learning. Recontextualization requires that the mind first unlearns old connections that were based on misconceptions or on irrelevant features. For example, students must first understand that not all numbers represent discrete entities before they can learn fractions as ratios and proportions.

How can teachers foster this recontextualization process? Consider the dialogue in a 3rd grade classroom:

Teacher: *Is one-half a lot, or just a little?*

Student L: *It is a little, because it is not even one.*

Student R: *It is a little, because 10 or a million is a lot, and a half is very little.*

Student D: *A half is little because it is when one is cut in half.*

Teacher: [showing a packaging box of a 5" individual pizza] *Is one-half of this pizza a lot or a little?*

Student M: *A little. I can eat two of those.*

Student L: *A little.*

Teacher: [showing a packaging box of a 10" family-size supreme pizza] *And a half of this?*

Student D: *This is a lot.*

Student R: *A lot.*

Teacher: *So, is half a lot or a little?*

Student W: *It depends if it is a big or a small pizza.*

Student L: *It is relative to the whole.*

Teacher: *Excellent. You used the word relative* [writes RELATIVE on the board]. *The size of the half is relative to the size of a whole. If the whole is large, the half of the whole is also large. If the whole is small, the half is small. The size of the part is relative to the size of the whole.*

Teacher: *Can you give an example of a part of a whole that is very large?*

Student Y: *Yes, three-quarters of the supreme pizza.*

Teacher: *OK. We have an example with pizza, now with something else.*

[Silence. The teacher waits.]

Student B: *A half of the universe is like billions of stars.*

Teacher: *Excellent. This is a very thoughtful example.*

Student R: *A half of the people in the whole world.*

Teacher: *Good, now examples from your daily life.*

Student W: *I cannot drink a half a bottle of milk, because it's too much . . .*

In this example, L's case demonstrates a meaningful generalization. Compare her initial determination that a half "is a little, because it is not even one" to her later conclusion that the quantitative value of a half "is relative to the whole." R's case demonstrates recontextualization with his example (counting his initial response) of a half that is "big." The teacher facilitated both meaningful inductions and recontextualizations by questioning and probing. Note that there was a pause in the otherwise lively discussion before the first examples for the new concept were generated by the students. This pause reflects the cognitive challenge of recontextualization and the importance of teacher mediation.

Consider the example illustrated in Figure 2.12 (see p. 38).

Independently, teachers must encourage students to identify applications for new concepts. Teachers need to devote time and direct effort to engage students in this process. Because the value of a concept is determined by the variety of its applications, teachers should encourage students to find different and varied

Figure 2.12

Recontextualizing the Concept of the Coefficient
as Slope and Intercept by Comparing and Contrasting

a) $y = -X + 5$

b) $y = X$

c) $y = -2X - 2$

d) $y = -X - 2$

e) $y = -X$

f) $y = -2$

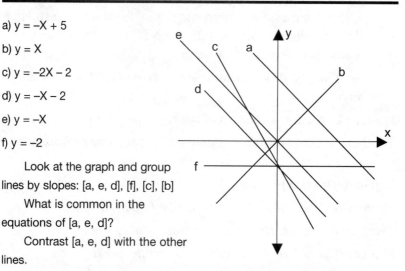

Look at the graph and group lines by slopes: [a, e, d], [f], [c], [b]

What is common in the equations of [a, e, d]?

Contrast [a, e, d] with the other lines.

Now look within (contrast) the group of lines [a, e, d]. How are the lines different?

Look at the equations that represent these lines. How are they different?

examples. Teachers can facilitate the search for variable applications by directing students to specific domains—such as shopping, design, or sports—or to other academic fields—such as geography, science, and the arts. To this end, teachers can effectively use cooperative learning (Cooperative Learning Center at the University of Minnesota, www.clcrc.com/index.html#essays).

Ms. Appleton's middle school class completed the geometry unit on Area and Perimeter. Her next goal was for her students to recontextualize their newly learned geometric concepts of area and perimeter through applications of their own. Ms. Appleton explained to her class that they would be working in groups of three to apply area and perimeter to a design or problem of their choice. Their assignment was to prepare a presentation to be made in class in two weeks. Ms. Appleton told her students that they could use the resources in the classroom, the library, or any of four Internet sites she had identified.

Ms. Appleton divided her class into groups of three. Every group agreed on the individual role and responsibility of each of its members. Ms. Appleton met with each group periodically to monitor their progress and assess their understanding.

At the end of two weeks Ms. Appleton's students presented projects that included fencing, carpeting, painting, and stadium capacity. Each group provided the teacher with a journal of their "mathematical thinking."

Finding particular applications for a concept should not be considered an end in itself. It can provide the means by which learners actually field-test the concept they have developed. Teachers should make certain that students examine the relevance of each example or its incongruity with the new concept they have learned. Is it always true, or in what conditions is it not?

5. Realization

Consider the case of 14-year-old Chad, a very intelligent (gifted) young man who was failing school. Chad's teachers held different opinions of his abilities, and he had different preferences for his teachers. His performance was inconsistent, even within a subject area. In Chad's strong opinion, academic success has nothing to do with being intelligent. To him, all that succeeding in school requires is "cloning the teacher." Many students are like Chad. They, too, find academic learning to be a mundane, "reproductory" process, because they do not realize the importance and applicability of what they learn beyond the school walls.

The ultimate test of learning lies in the volitional act of realizing that what has been learned is applicable across the curriculum and in everyday life. Such learning depends on teachers' persistent expectations that students seek out such realization, on consistent support across the school curriculum for promotion of this important process, and on the expectations and support of parents or caregivers at home.

Realization validates learning and turns students' experiences in the classroom into meaningful and useful activities. Schools must be environments that reinforce intelligent student life; develop a system of values and standards that supports learning; and maintain an atmosphere that fosters student realization of new concepts. In such an environment, teachers plan opportunities to apply new concepts across the curriculum. In such an environment, students are held accountable for the realization of their mathematics learning across different academic areas and beyond school (Fullan, 2000). What should schools be like to foster such environments?

Schools must be places where teachers and parents share goals and assess progress. For instance, a school can adapt some form of the Japanese practice of lesson study that involves groups of teachers working together on developing goals, studying student difficulties with particular concepts, and exploring different applications (Watanabe, 2002). A school can organize cross-discipline staff meetings that allow teachers to identify critical concepts, explore possible learning experiences, and develop strategies that reinforce applications of new concepts across the academic disciplines. Schools can also involve parents in these meetings and decisions.

Summary

The Glenn Commission took a clear position on the current state of mathematics education. They wrote, "Students are crippled by content limited to 'what?' They get only a little bit about the 'how?' (or 'how else?'), and not nearly enough about the 'why?'" (*National Commission on Mathematics and Science Teaching for the 21st Century,* 2000, p. 21). If instruction should foster the understanding of mathematics concepts and the ability to apply them, then it must follow the leads of current cognitive research on learning, not the fads that favor quick learning time, fast memory work, and teachers working from scripts. Teachers must identify the core mathematics concepts and decide the sequence of instruction, considering which concepts students have already learned. Teachers must also consider the requirements and constraints. Once they consider all these factors, teachers must plan Concept-Rich Instruction.

Concept-Rich Instruction neither tells students the what, why, and how of concepts nor leaves students to self-directed inquiry. Concept-Rich Instruction requires the teacher to guide the students' investigation of experiences related to the concept and to help the students make the connections that lead to a full understanding of the concept. As in real life, the concepts of school mathematics are embedded in science, social studies, technology, business, shopping, sports, the arts, and literature. Concepts are embedded in every problem to which mathematics is applied. Teachers must help students develop these concepts. They must be responsive to the learning needs of students and provide effective guidance. Within limited time frames, teachers must identify target concepts, provide sufficient practice, help students decontextualize and induce their meaning, help students recontextualize, and coach students in realizing them. In contrast, redundant and rudimentary instruction is not effective and is more time-consuming.

School faculty can create a community of learners that is supported by a commitment to a restructured curriculum. They must structure a curriculum that is centered on concepts and allows the time for each teacher to use the instructional strategies that engage all students in the development of the concepts and permits development of appropriate attitudes. As a result, students will better realize mathematics concepts across the curriculum.

Chapter 3

Misconceptions

After a review of conceptual development, it is appropriate to examine how misconceptions occur and why certain types of conceptual errors are so common in school mathematics. Without such considerations, teachers cannot help their students replace their misconceptions with new concepts.

Indeed, conceptualization often means a correction of prior misconception. Therefore, as they follow the essential steps of Concept-Rich Instruction, teachers often encounter the challenge—at times remarkable challenge—of altering students' misconceptions. To be effective, teachers must anticipate, understand, and know how misconceptions are replaced by the formal concepts. This chapter focuses on typical students' misconceptions in mathematics, how they develop, and how they change through effective instruction.

Instruction that aims at altering misconceptions must be based on teachers' understanding of the underlying cognitive structures. Research shows that informed teachers alter their students' misconceptions by adjusting the sequence of instruction where necessary and by choosing different experiences with various applications of the target concepts (Derry, Levin, Osana, & Jones, 1998; Lehman, Lempert, & Nisbett, 1988;

Nisbett, Fong, Lehman, & Cheng, 1987). Uninformed teachers tend to explain misconceptions as a result of laziness, carelessness, or incapability and do not adjust instruction to meet the real learning needs. Their classrooms feature a mismatch of perceptions. Misconceptions reflect the sense that students make of what they learn, and mathematical concepts reflect the sense that teachers make of what they want to teach.

The notion of misconception is based on the hypothesis of conflicting logics: the "objective logic" that is the concepts, and the "psycho-logic" that is the misconceptions. Constructivists believe that the psycho-logic has a significant function in conceptual development. Students do not "forget" their misconceptions when they are presented with formal concepts. They first understand mathematics from their misconceived perspective, and as they progress they gradually refine and reorganize their knowledge. Thus, constructivists consider misconceptions as states and refer to them in developmental terms like "preconception," "primitive alternative frameworks," or "naive intuitive ideas." Constructivists may consider as misconceptions those false ideas that students develop because of careless instruction that are not altered in subsequent learning. For example, consider the case of 3rd grader Kevin, who thought that right angles were always made up of horizontal and vertical lines. When Kevin learned about right angles, his teacher always drew them on the board as the angle between horizontal and vertical lines. His classmate, Jamahl, disagreed. He thought that only half of Kevin's drawings of right angles were correct—the other half of them were in fact "left angles." Concept-Rich Instruction is largely based on the constructivist theory.

Preconceptions are more common than misconceptions. For example, when a teacher asked 4th grader Melissa to draw a "perfect" rectangle that was 10 centimeters long and 5 centimeters wide, she meticulously drew a 9-inch by 4-inch rectangle. It was evident that Melissa did not pay much attention to the units of measurement; however, because she systematically started measuring from one and not from zero, we thought she also had some problems with the concept of "zero." It turned out that she had never been formally taught how to measure length and that she still held on to the misconception of zero as "nothing—therefore, there is nothing there."

Concept-Rich Instruction views procedural knowledge and conceptual knowledge as interrelated and assumes that at least some errors in procedures are rooted in misconceptions. Melissa's case also illustrates the interrelationship between conceptual and procedural understanding.

Systematic Errors

Some student errors in mathematics are systematic. Cognitive scientists who refer to such errors as "bugs" have shown that such errors are neither random nor "sloppy" (Brown & Burton, 1978). Programs that are based on research in cognition—as well as research in computer technology, artificial intelligence, and linguistics—can simulate learning processes and predict exactly the typical errors. Best known among these programs are Error Analysis Diagnosis in Mathematics (EADIM), Sierra (VanLehn of Carnegie Mellon University), and Mind Bugs (Gleitman, Carey, Newport, & Spelke, 1989). These programs can produce the common systematic errors and predict when and how those errors will occur before students' work first shows them. Good teachers also see and recognize systematic errors. They recognize systematic errors in the work of even the most consistently organized, reflective, and articulate students. When teachers examine systematic errors carefully, they can see that the errors are reasoned and not capricious. They are either preconceptions or false, naive intuitions.

Preconceptions

Conceptualization is a learning process that involves assimilation of new experiences into an expanding structure of cognitive and conceptual schemata. The relative levels of conceptual understanding reflect a degree of flexibility and decontextualization.

Throughout the learning process, preconceptions represent either overgeneralization or undergeneralization of mathematical concepts. Examples of both kinds of preconceptions in the areas of arithmetic, algebra, geometry, and probability and statistics are listed in Figure 3.1.

These examples of preconceptions are common in the classroom. Although in general such student preconceptions are ultimately replaced by the true mathematical concepts, instruction that is reciprocal and well-informed by the learning process can accelerate it.

Figure 3.1

Preconceptions in School Arithmetic, Algebra, Geometry, and Probability and Statistics

Topic of School Mathematics	Preconceptions
Geometry (measurement/ number-sense)	The number concept is restricted to natural numbers. Given a ruler, a student would consider the starting point for the measurement of length at one, not at zero on the measuring device.
Geometry	Orientation is relevant to the definition of geometrical forms.
Geometry	Angles are influenced by the orientation of lines in space and by their length.
Arithmetic (integers)	Primary grade students believe that there is no number smaller than zero.
Arithmetic (fractions)	Multiplication is always successive addition.
Arithmetic (fractions)	Fractions always represent part-whole relationships.
Pre-algebra	The equality sign represents a command for executing a series of arithmetic operation— not as a sign for a relationship of "equality."
Pre-algebra (letters represent unspecified quantities)	A great number of students ignore the letters, replace them with specific numerical values, or regard them as names or measurement labels.
Algebra (structure)	Answers cannot include operation signs. A student does not understand how, in algebra, two perceptually different expressions can be equal.

Undergeneralizations

Undergeneralization is manifested in limited understanding and limited ability to apply concepts. Limited understanding describes much of the state of student knowledge at any time throughout the development of mathematical ideas. A few examples can illustrate how such limited understanding is detrimental to the conception of key mathematical ideas.

The case of rational numbers is probably among the most problematic for middle school students. Many research studies indicate that middle school students understand rational numbers only as part-whole relationships (e.g., Hert, 1981; Kerslake, 1986). In fact, the interpretation of fractions as part-whole relationships constitutes only a subconcept or one way of understanding of rational numbers. Other subconcepts of rational numbers include fractions that feature ratios, quotients, measures, and operators. For example, a student with limited understanding of rational numbers may not consider 6 : 7 the same as 6/7 because the former was developed in the context of learning about ratios and the latter in the context of learning about division (operator). A student may not understand 3/4 as "odds" (whole-whole or part-part relationships) because he understands ratio only as a part-whole relationship. A student may not understand a given fraction as a measure, or a number in its own right, because she has learned it as a part-whole relationship.

Conceptualizing rational numbers involves both differentiation and integration of these subconcepts. Before the full concept of rational numbers develops, students always undergeneralize it. Instruction on the number system must always respond to problems of undergeneralization because presuppositions regarding the discreteness in the number system inhibit the more general understanding (Gelman, 2000; Lipton & Spelke, 2003).

Another known area of great difficulty for students who had not generalized the formal mathematical structures when they learned arithmetic involves the transition from arithmetical to algebraic thinking. The quantitative intuition that helps these students understand arithmetic becomes useless as they transition from arithmetic to algebra. These students cannot operate upon unknown numerical facts; they cannot recognize particular instances in general forms and cannot apply general forms to particular instances. For example, these students cannot make sense of equations like "2x + 3 = 8 – x" because "2x + 3" does not make "8 – x." They do not accept as equal such expressions as (a – b)(a + b) and (a + b)(a – b), ab and ba, or a(b + c) and ab + ac because they cannot "check to see if it is true." Generalizing mathematical ideas is a major challenge, and expressing these generalizations or rendering them into the formal language of algebra is another. Consider, for example, the generalization of the distributive property, as illustrated in Figure 3.2.

With all the challenges involved in generalization and abstraction, effective instruction must proceed gradually and thoughtfully from the manipulation of arithmetical facts to mental and symbolic objects (Mason, 1993).

Overgeneralizations

Faulty interpretations lead to faulty generalizations in yet a different way—as in the case of overgeneralization and application of poorly understood concepts and rules where they are not relevant. Middle school teachers see this problem very clearly as their students encounter the extension of the number system from natural numbers to integers and from whole numbers to

Figure 3.2
Generalizing Mathematical Ideas

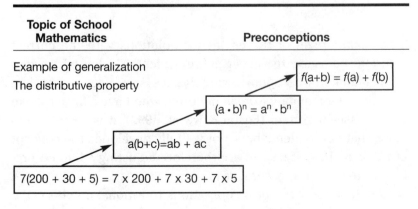

Topic of School Mathematics	Preconceptions

Example of generalization
The distributive property

$f(a+b) = f(a) + f(b)$

$(a \cdot b)^n = a^n \cdot b^n$

$a(b+c) = ab + ac$

$7(200 + 30 + 5) = 7 \times 200 + 7 \times 30 + 7 \times 5$

rational numbers, the confusions of operations with numbers and scientific notations, and the transition from arithmetic to algebra.

Students typically overgeneralize that "you cannot have less than nothing" until they encounter integers and find out that this generalization does not work. They typically overgeneralize that products are always bigger than their factors until they have to make sense of smaller products in the case of fractional numbers (Bell, Fischbein, & Greer, 1984; Fischbein, Deri, Nello, & Marino, 1985). From their limited experience with power notation in its whole number manifestation, students overgeneralize that power represents multiplication. Raising x to the power of ½ makes absolutely no sense to them because they cannot understand "half an x multiplied together" (Tall, 2002).

Overgeneralization is also manifested in mathematical operations. For example, typically found among 3rd grade students is the error (bug) involving multidigit subtraction, where one of the digits in the minuend (the top number) is zero:

(1)	507 -134 433		(4)	503 -421 222
(2)	708 -459 351		(5)	189 -133 56
(3)	606 -127 521		(6)	439 -345 114

A comparison of the erroneous solutions with the correct solutions helps locate the bug in the student's dealing with a zero in the minuend where "borrowing" is necessary. Because this bug is not common among Korean children, who have a firmer grasp of the base-10 system (Fuson & Kwon, 1992), it is easy to conclude that our students have not yet fully developed the concept of the base-10 system and are therefore adjusting a limited procedure to the more general case.

As they apply the basic operations to rational numbers, the majority of 4th and 5th grade students understand very little of what the quantities symbols represent and make frequent and nonsensical errors when they apply the false rules they learned by rote (Resnick et al., 1989). Even worse, many students are indifferent about the irrational results of their mathematical operations. For example, overgeneralizing that addition and subtraction always "work just like" they do with multidigit whole numbers leads them to systematic errors in the addition and subtraction of fractions. As they try to subtract a fraction from a smaller fraction, students may decompose any whole to 100 parts, regardless of the value of the denominator:

$$8\tfrac{1}{4} - 7\tfrac{3}{5} = 8\tfrac{5}{20} - 7\tfrac{12}{20} = 7\tfrac{105}{20} - 7\tfrac{12}{20}$$

In other instances, students compute a common denominator whenever they multiply fractions, thus overgeneralizing the rule that "works" for the addition of fractions. When they add and subtract decimal fractions, they use a rule they learned with whole numbers—to "line up the numbers on the right," being absolutely indifferent to the nonsensical conclusion that the sum of 1.5 and 0.46 is 0.61 (Hiebert & Wearne, 1986).

Early on, different levels of conceptualization may not be manifested in the students' work, but over time the different levels become quite evident. At some point in students' education, the shallow understanding of mathematical concepts becomes transparent enough for teachers to become alarmed by the overgeneralizations that hinder the students' transition to algebra.

For example, overgeneralization of algebraic forms like $a(b + c) = a!b + a!c$ leads students to a false conclusion that $a + (b!c) = (a + b) \bullet (a + c)$. Overgeneralization of superficial symbolic structures (application of the same procedures to symbols that look alike) leads such students to attempt to solve $(x - 1) 2 = 1$ as if it were $(x - 1) 2 = 0$, and then "correct the results" by adding 1. The internal cognitive conflicts between overgeneralized ideas and a different new experience result either in constructive conceptual development, or in "taking the line of less resistance" by rote learning of new "rules." Unfortunately, the most prevalent case is rote learning. In other words, in teachers' attempts to facilitate conceptual understanding, they will likely find students' desire to *know the rules* to be stronger than their desire to *understand* them.

In the cases of students who have not fully developed concepts and processes, explicitly telling the students the correct answers, concepts, or procedure is a futile exercise of instruction. For example, it does not make sense to forbid finger counting when children prefer it over other strategies for solving arithmetic problems; it does not make sense to "show" students the correct operations with fractions and decimals when they do not understand the rules; and algebraic concepts do not make more sense to students simply because they are "retaught." Students generally abandon their preconcepts naturally as they reflect upon new experiences and figure out more efficient strategies. Therefore, teachers should engage the students in a sequence of learning experiences that can lead them from the preconceptions to the canonical mathematics view. Teachers should always lead the learning process as gradually as possible from preconceptions to deeper conceptual understanding.

Counterintuitive Concepts

As evident in the works of great scientists and artists, intuition plays a significant role in scientific discovery and the arts. In fact, experts argue that intuition is involved in all their decisions (e.g., Miller, 1996). Although it is composed of most of our mental activity, intuition is not a conscious, analytical—that is, logical, sequential, step-by-step, and reasoned—process of thinking (Bunge, 1962). The case of mathematics deserves a somewhat different consideration than the sciences.

Mathematical concepts for the most part are outcomes of conscious, analytical processes of thinking. Intuition plays a role only in the basic beliefs of mathematics that are (subconsciously) true by insistence, not by proof, and are referred to as mathematical axioms (postulates). While intuition is important to solving problems in mathematics, sometimes mathematical deductions appear counterintuitive. In reference to counterintuitive concepts, two areas of mathematics come immediately to mind. One is the area of non-Euclidean geometry, and the other is the mathematics of probability and statistics.

The Case of Non-Euclidean Geometry

From popular expert views and the fact that the basic postulates of Euclidean geometry were first established over 2 millennia ago and did not change until the 19th century, it appears that the human perception of space and time is intuitively compatible with the basic postulates of Euclidean geometry (see Figure 3.3). This assumption implies that geometries that are not based on the basic postulates of Euclid are counterintuitive. Indeed, the negation of Euclid's fifth (parallel) postulate and the logical consequence led to great controversy and eventually to the development of a range of non-Euclidean geometries that are characterized by curvatures, such as hyperbolic geometry or elliptic geometry.

Collectively, these five assumptions are referred to as "Euclid's postulates," or "Euclid's axioms." The fifth postulate is called "Euclid's parallel postulate," or the "parallelism axiom."

The negation of the fifth Euclid postulate, asserting that different lines that share a given point and at the same time are parallel to a given line do exist, has led to the deduction of non-Euclidean theorems and implications (e.g., the angle sum in a triangle in hyperbolic geometry is less than 180 degrees) that are counterintuitive to those who learn non-Euclidean geometries. This case of counterintuitive geometry concepts is interesting in terms of illustrating where naive intuitions conflict with mathematical concepts, although this example is relevant only to the mathematics learning of high school advanced placement mathematics students. The counterintuitive mathematical concepts involved in probability and statistics are relevant to most of our students.

Figure 3.3
Euclid's Five Postulates

1. We can draw a [unique] line segment between any two points.

2. Any line segment can be continued indefinitely.

3. A circle can be described with any center and radius.

4. Any two right angles are congruent.

5. (Playfair's form) Given a line *m* and a point *P* not on *m*, there exists a unique line *n* through *P* that does not intersect *m*.

The Case of Probability and Statistics

Most students come to school with faulty naive intuitions—misconceptions—about probability and statistics that are reinforced by social stereotypes and idiosyncratic observations. For example, children, and even adults sometimes, tend to have a deterministic view of uncertain future situations. They intuitively tend to predict the outcome of a single trial, not the probability of its occurrence (Konold, 1989). This naive intuition gives rise to seven known misconceptions that are summarized in Figure 3.4.

False intuition challenges all the students who are introduced to probability and statistics. Although the National Council of Teachers of Mathematics standards establish that all students learn the basic concepts of this discipline of mathematics, as many as three-fourths of 12th grade students in 1999 have not received any instruction in this subject. It is important that all mathematics teachers understand the implications of these counterintuitive concepts. Policymakers and experts believe that the full implementation of probability and statistics in school mathematics is just a matter of short time (Shaughnessy & Zawojewski, 1999).

False, naive intuitions constitute one possible source of systematic errors in the conceptual understanding of mathematics. The more significant role of false intuitions in mathematical thinking, however, involves difficulties with solving problems.

Errors as Instructional Tools

The instructional importance of detailed analyses of concepts and their procedural implications is clear. It is also clear that teachers can anticipate most, if not all, of the known misconceptions students hold and can identify them in systematic errors in students' work. Some research already exists that shows that instruction can effectively alter typical misconception (Derry et al., 1998; Lehman et al., 1988; Nisbett et al., 1987). This chapter focuses on this research as it emphasizes the instructional import of conceptual errors—the "seventh sense" of Concept-Rich Instruction.

Figure 3.4

Typical Counterintuitive Notions in Probability and Statistics

Misconception	Explanation	Example
The representative fallacy	A tendency to over-estimate the likelihood of events based on representative cases rather than a whole set of data.	When considering sequences of the births of boys (B) and girls (G) in a family, the sequence BBGGBG is rated more probable than the sequence BGBBBG. The sequences are in fact equally likely.
Insensitivity to sample size, stereotyping *Resistant to change.*	The probabilities of events appear higher than they actually are if they receive more exposure (e.g., by the media).	The major reason for stereotyping based on such factors as racial and ethnic groups.
The availability heuristic *Resistant to change.*	The estimate of likeli-hood is based on how easily events are recalled from past experiences.	Based on bad service once at a restaurant, we may decide not to visit that restaurant any more.
The "gamblers' fallacy" (sometimes referred to as the "we are due" effect)	Recent events have more weight on the conception of the likelihood of future events.	In flipping a coin, one of who flips heads 10 times in a row believes that tails is more likely to turn up next. In fact, it is as likely as heads.
The conjunction fallacy	When the probability of compounds, p(A and B), are thought to be more likely than the individual probability, p(A), because p(B) is more probable than A alone.	Considering "Bill plays jazz for a hobby," less probable than "Bill is an accountant who plays jazz for a hobby." In fact, it is the opposite.
Simple and compound events—Equiprobability bias *Resistant to change.*	As a result of misunder-standing the sample space, similar proba-bilities are assigned to two different events.	The probability of draw-ing 6-6 on dice appears to be the same as the probability of drawing a 5-6. In fact, the latter is twice as likely.
Time axis fallacy—"The Falk Phenomenon" *Resistant to change.*	The assumption that the knowledge of an event's outcome cannot be used to determine the probability of the occurrence of a previous event.	If two machines have known defect rates, people affected by this fallacy cannot understand that it is possible to determine the probability that a defective product came from a particular machine, and the probability that it came from the other machine.

Sources: Borovcnik & Bentz, 1991; Kahneman, Slovic, & Tversky, 1982; Scholz, 1991. From *Mediating Probability and Statistics: A Manual for Successful Mathematics Teaching* by Meir Ben-Hur. © 2004 by International Renewal Institute, Inc., Glencoe, Illinois. Reprinted with permission for worldwide and electronic rights.

Teachers generally welcome my visits to their classrooms. Once in a while, I show up and find myself politely escorted to a different classroom than the one I intended to visit, which is involved in testing or a school activity of some sort. Knowing the reality of schools, I am never surprised. I was utterly surprised one day, however, when Ms. M., who always anticipates my visits with animated pleasure, suggested that I should visit another classroom that day instead of hers because, in her words, she did not have anything to teach—she intended to "just go over the last week's exam." To Ms. M.'s surprise, I proposed that I model a "going over the last week's exam" lesson. We went to the classroom together and I delivered a lesson that turned out to be one of my best. It focused on the students' errors. (I termed those errors "brave-students" errors as I "allowed" only the brave students to present, and try to defend, their errors.) From that lesson and many lessons that followed that visit, I learned the incredible instructional value of student errors.

Student errors are among the most underutilized resources in education. Errors are definitely "available" in groups of 20 and 30 students who operate at the edge of their mathematical competence on many different assignments, quizzes, and tests. The errors are routinely recognized and acknowledged by teachers. If teachers are not careful enough to recognize and indicate students' errors, then the students automatically think they erred if they notice that their answers are different from what the teacher or other students present as correct answers; students believe that there is always one and only one correct answer. Errors rarely receive any other treatment than the deserved "correction," however. Errors are commonly perceived by both teachers and students as unfortunate mistakes and therefore deserving of no other attention than acknowledgment. This common perception is particularly wrong in the case of errors that are rooted in misconceptions. In fact, these errors deserve the utmost teacher attention.

Research indicates that student misconceptions are resistant to change. Changing misconceptions is not as simple as bringing errors to students' awareness. Misconceptions are altered only by *assimilating* conflicting experiences—a reflective analytical process. Thus, if students cannot alter their misconceptions by themselves because they do not reflect upon the thinking that led to errors, then they "alter" their conflict by selectively choosing some parts and ignoring the problematic parts of the process so that their experiences remain consistent with their misconceptions. Worse, many students "learn" to hold multiple and often contradictory mathematical ideas at the same time (Konold, 1989, 1991; Shaugnessy, 1993). These students answer correctly on examinations and quizzes but continue to operate outside the formal situations according to their preconceptions (De Lisi & Golbeck, 1999). Teachers must mediate and facilitate the reflective process that leads to reconceptualization.

Six Instructional Principles for Conceptual Remediation

Concept-Rich Instruction is based on Vygotsky's socioculturist teaching on the value of thoughtful communication with and among people to the development of their knowledge and cognitive skills (Feuerstein & Rand, 1997; Vygotsky, 1978). The basic premise of Concept-Rich Instruction is that the context of classroom discussion imposes on its participants a need to report and answer questions verbally, challenging all who are involved to form, reflect upon, examine, and revise their differing ideas. When classroom discussions focus on students' work, particularly students' errors, teachers not only can inquire, analyze, and try to understand how students erred, but also assess possible misconceptions. As students become aware of their errors and continue to communicate their reasoning effectively, the ensuing discussions provide opportunity-rich contexts for guidance in the correction of misconceptions.

Reuven Feuerstein refers to learning as advocated by Concept-Rich Instruction as "mediated learning experience," or MLE (Feuerstein & Rand, 1997). One of three critical parameters that describe what teachers do when they mediate learning is the reciprocal relationship between the teacher (mediator) and the learner. This parameter ensures that mediation is always responsive to emerging learning needs. As Feuerstein teaches, and as Concept-Rich Instruction espouses, for the relationship to be reciprocal, teachers must be flexible. They must be ready to modify their lessons to include objectives that relate to emerging needs, engage their struggling students with alternative representations of new concepts, teach the formal vocabulary effectively, provide more learning experiences as needed, and facilitate reflective interactions among learners. All of these practices are examined in the six instructional principles for conceptual remediation that follow.

1. Reciprocity

Altering mathematical misconceptions is largely a responsive process that occurs in the context of reflective communication between students and teacher or among students. Active participants always share goals and anticipate learning. This responsive process is built on a trusting relationship. Collaborators explicate reasons, resolve differences, listen to one another's points of view, receive feedback, and reach consensus. At the successful end, all the collaborators are transformed in different ways (see Figure 3.5). Even when it involves a teacher and a student, both are transformed as a result of the process.

Clearly, there are several possibilities for something to go wrong in this process. If the process breaks down, the teacher will not achieve the desired outcome. Therefore, throughout the dialogue, the teacher must maintain the students' interest in the discussion, be very careful to listen to what students say, watch how they react, and ensure that they are comfortable with the conclusions.

2. Flexibility

As a teacher identifies potentially confusing conceptual areas or misconceptions, he may have to change his original curricular decisions. He may have to go back to improve students' prerequisite understanding, stay longer with a topic and just add learning activities, or change the order of subsequent lessons to incorporate additional or different objectives. Merely "covering" a topic on a set schedule may not happen. These kinds of decisions

Figure 3.5

Reciprocity Between Teacher and Student

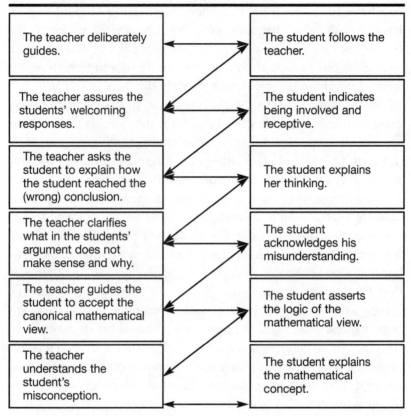

are very common in Concept-Rich Instruction. Take for example the case of decimal fractions.

Many of the errors students make when they attempt to add decimal fractions show that they apply to fractions poorly understood rules about the long addition of natural numbers. For example, a teacher may find that when students add decimal fractions, some align numbers on the right. This poor understanding leads the students to get 0.135, or 1.35 when adding 6.3 and 0.72. A teacher who recognizes this problem responds by engaging her students in explaining why they should add decimals in a way that appears to be different from the addition of whole numbers. In the course of this discussion, she finds that some students misunderstood the decimal form of fractions altogether. She decides that more time is needed to review the topic than she initially planned, and the classroom discussion will have to go even further back to what the student should have learned the previous year. In this review process, the teacher not only deals with the particular case of addition with decimals, but probes the deeper meaning of addition to reveal what is common among the apparently different applications.

At the same time that teachers respond to a particular misconception in one area of mathematics, they may decide to help their students to form important conceptual linkages with other areas. In this case, the teacher would have to differentiate and integrate similar subject materials that happen in different textbook chapters and in different places in the mathematics course. For example, the concept that adding is meaningful only when it is applied to like terms, which underlies the already-known case of addition with whole numbers (based upon the place value system of whole numbers), is also applicable to adding decimals and adding other fractional forms (common denominator); to solving problems that involve adding different units of measurement; and to adding algebraic expressions. Thus, the teacher who helps his students make the conceptual connections not only helps them correct a misconception, but also expands their understanding of the mathematical concept of addition in preparation for future learning.

In many cases, as teachers identify misconceptions, they realize that changing the original curricular decisions may involve more than one lesson. In these cases, teachers modify their plans for a series of subsequent lessons. This form of great flexibility features the reflective practice that characterizes Concept-Rich Instruction. This was the case in Ms. Smith's classroom.

Ms. Smith's Example of a Modified Lesson

Ms. Smith realized that her students have a very inconsistent understanding of polynomials and that she needed to help her students to make connections between algebra and arithmetic. She decided to modify a lesson she had planned on factoring polynomials. She started by setting up her new objectives. Then she used a pre-test to survey her students' understanding and a post-test to evaluate the lesson. The lesson included cooperative small-group work on a list of tasks. These tasks were designed to lead the students to discover the factors of quadratic polynomials. In her new lesson plan, Ms. Smith indicated the modifications she had made to the lesson. She engaged her students in problem solving by asking them to use the "cover-up approach" with negative factors. She asked her students to investigate conjectures using "perfect square trinomials" and "difference of squares" and included an activity that would help them make connections. Then she guided her students in using factoring to solve quadratic equations in word problems dealing with the dimensions of a picture frame.

In this modified lesson, one can see the increased complexity in the work she required of her students, the connection of ideas across different situations, and the potential for a more profound understanding of the mathematical concepts. Her modified lesson indicates her flexibility and her professional reflections.

3. Alternative Mental Representations

Mental representation, or imagery, precedes understanding. Representation frees our reliance on perception and allows us to embody meaning in imagery. Representation of numeration involves visual images and symbols; in geometry it involves language and icons; and in algebra it involves graphic and symbolic forms. Thus, representation relieves students from the need to operate solely upon what they see and what they can physically manipulate. It allows students to discriminate—to compare and classify input information—and enables their thinking to explain reality. Understanding mathematical ideas involves mental representations that affect each other.

As in the general case of conceptualization in mathematics, teachers must help students alter misconceptions through modeling mathematical ideas in alternative forms—oral, written, pictorial, graphic, and symbolic. For example, when a 5th grade teacher saw that one of her students continued to represent fractions only as part-whole relationships by consistently drawing a pie chart to feature his understanding of any fractions, she challenged her class to draw and share different pictures of a given fraction (1/3).

She knew that students should be able to generate mathematical operations as well as objects.

Understanding division with fractions is an area that teachers find problematic. For example, Figures 3.6, 3.7, and 3.8 show understanding and generalizing division with fractions through at least three different representations.

Figure 3.6
The Measurement Model of Division

This model provides a justification for the algorithm used in the division of fractions.

Find the whole of which a half is $1\frac{3}{4}$

To know the whole, given the part ($1\frac{3}{4}$) and the fact that the part is $\frac{1}{2}$ of the whole, one must first ask how many of this part will fit the whole. The answer is 2 (which is the reciprocal). Then one multiplies the value of the part by the reciprocal ($1\frac{3}{4} \times 2$). In short: $1\frac{3}{4} \div \frac{1}{2} = 1\frac{3}{4} \times 2$.

From *Investigating the Big Idea of Arithmetic: A Manual for Successful Mathematics Teaching* by Meir Ben-Hur. © 2004 by International Renewal Institute, Inc., Glencoe, Illinois. Reprinted with permission for worldwide and electronic rights.

Figure 3.7
The Partitive Model of Division

This partitive model matches the naive understanding of division. Here one applies spatial reasoning to solve the problem. This model, however, does not easily "explain" the computation.

Find how many halves are included in $1\frac{3}{4}$

Here the answer $3\frac{1}{2}$ is visually appealing.

Another example:

How many cakes can be baked with $1\frac{3}{4}$ pounds of flour if each cake requires $\frac{1}{2}$ pound of flour?

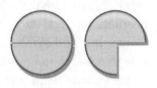

$$1\frac{3}{4} \div \frac{1}{2} = 3\frac{1}{2}$$

From *Investigating the Big Idea of Arithmetic: A Manual for Successful Mathematics Teaching* by Meir Ben-Hur. © 2004 by International Renewal Institute, Inc., Glencoe, Illinois. Reprinted with permission for worldwide and electronic rights.

Figure 3.8
The Factor and Product Model of Division

This model is commonly seen in multidimensional graphs, where the factors are independent of one another and connected only conceptually (distance is a function of time and speed). Consider such cases as "work problems," "motion problems," or "momentum or balance" problems as they appear in achievement tests. All of these problems require an abstract notion of division (and multiplication).

From *Investigating the Big Idea of Arithmetic: A Manual for Successful Mathematics Teaching* by Meir Ben-Hur. © 2004 by International Renewal Institute, Inc., Glencoe, Illinois. Reprinted with permission for worldwide and electronic rights.

Understanding the alternative representations and the resulting general notion of division permits an easier transfer for use with a variety of problems.

As teachers try to change student misconceptions in mathematics, they must also distinguish between internal (mental) and external representations. Although students clearly benefit from their experience with new external representations of ideas, the goal of Concept-Rich Instruction is to develop a volitional act of representing ideas mentally. For example, students may learn about algebraic functions with the help of graphic calculators or algebra tiles, but eventually algebraic ideas that are abstract can be represented and communicated only in symbols. In this respect, the perceptual awareness is the arithmetic and the visual images that arithmetic generates, but the conceptual awareness that is algebra is represented in the universal symbols that constitute the means by which educated people can think and communicate algebraically. Research shows that low-achieving algebra students fail to "see" these relational algebraic characteristics in the absence of external representations (Neuman & Schwarz, 2000). It implies that teachers should always consider manipulatives in arithmetic, graphs in algebra, and a range of other teaching devices in mathematics only as means for the development of internal representations. If the end result of teaching should be conceptualization and correction of misconceptions, then these devices should never be considered as ends to themselves.

4. Meta-cognitive Awareness

There is ample evidence that presenting cognitive challenges, and hoping this practice in itself will cause students to learn to reason, does not work (Costa, 2001). In mathematics education, it is also clear that although teachers may be keenly aware of the relationships among logic, mathematical concepts, and their applications, and between misconceptions and the resulting errors, many students still fail to clearly see these relationships. Consequently, many students do not independently alter their flawed logic and instead retain their misconceptions when they are presented with conflicting new evidence. Teachers must play a key role not only in correcting their students' misconceptions, but also in helping them learn from processes that resulted in the correction of their misconceptions. The research shows that instruction that promotes meta-learning and meta-knowledge strategies, particularly if such instruction begins in the early grades, produces students who are better learners and who acquire or retain significantly fewer misconceptions. Several instructional strategies are known to be effective. These include Reflection-in-Action, Feuerstein's mediated learning programs, deBono's programs, and Lipman's Philosophy for Children.

Reflection-in-Action

Reflection-in-Action is a practice that is commonly associated with teacher preparation. This reportedly very effective practice features elements that can be suitable for school students as well. Based on Schön's idea of learning (Schön, 1983), Reflection-in-Action involves thinking about reasons for what one says or does while learning about one's misconceptions. Reflection-in-Action is apparently more effective than reflecting *after* the learning has already occurred. Either way, reflecting involves stepping back from, mulling over, or tentatively exploring reasons. The following scenario displays the nature of Reflection-in-Action:

" . . .This was quite possibly because . . . Otherwise, . . ."

" . . .The problem here, I think, was that . . ."

" . . .Although it may be true that . . ."

" . . .On the one hand . . . yet on the other . . ."

" . . .In thinking back . . ."

" . . .I guess that this error made me aware of . . ."

Because school students may not be meta-cognitively aware, initially teachers may have to impose Reflection-in-Action in the classroom dialogue by questioning and probing.

" . . .Why was this possible? . . . How else? . . ."

" . . .What is the problem here? . . ."

" . . .Why did you change your mind? . . ."

" . . .How else? . . ."

" . . .How would you do it differently next time? . . ."

" . . .What did you learn from this error? . . ."

With time, as reflection becomes part of the classroom culture, Reflection-in-Action is likely to be increasingly internalized and initiated by students.

Mediation of Meta-cognitive Awareness as Modeled by deBono's, Lipman's, and Feuerstein's Cognitive Intervention Programs

In their design of the pioneering programs for the promotion of higher-level thinking skills in school children, Feuerstein, deBono, and Lipman realized the importance of emphasis on meta-cognitive functions (deBono, 1985; Feuerstein, 1980; Lipman, 1984). They understood that without teaching self-regulation, self-monitoring, and self-evaluation of cognitive processing, it is doubtful that much structural cognitive growth would be possible. Hence, although meta-cognitive awareness is a key feature of these programs, the goal is that over time students internalize strategies of self-learning and self-activated cognitive and meta-cognitive systems.

These programs create meta-cognitive awareness. Teachers are trained to challenge students to plan, monitor, and evaluate their work on the given programs' tasks. Meta-cognitive awareness develops as teachers regularly challenge their students to reflect upon application of the same processes and the same concepts that they identify in the classroom context in real-life problem-solving situations. In these programs, teachers learn to evaluate and improve their instruction in terms of

- Students' improved awareness of how they approach problems,
- Students' improved awareness of how they learn from their mistakes and successes,
- Students' improved perception of themselves as generators of information,
- Students' intrinsic motivation, and
- Students' transfer of learning from one situation or context to the next.

Among the three pioneering programs, research in Feuerstein's Instrumental Enrichment is the most comprehensive and establishes that these features of meta-cognitive awareness building are effective even with low-functioning students (Ben-Hur, 1994; Ellis, 2001; Mayer, 2000).

Graphic Organizers

Venn diagrams, concept mapping, tables, and new visual representations of knowledge are powerful tools for the development of meta-knowledge (knowledge about knowledge). These tools can help students understand new concepts, explore new conceptual relationships, connect new concepts with prior knowledge, and share knowledge and information. At the same time, when appropriately used, these tools provide an opportunity for teachers and students to identify misconceptions and find flaws in the cognitive structures that hold students' concepts together. Figure 3.9 provides an example of a concept map teachers can use in geometry classes.

Concept maps are tools for organizing knowledge into classes and categories (Novak, 1977, 1990). They depict concepts,

Figure 3.9
Concept Map

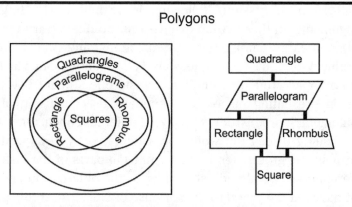

Polygons

From *Overcoming the Challenge of Geometry: A Manual for Successful Mathematics Teaching* by Meir Ben-Hur. © 2004 by International Renewal Institutes, Inc., Glencoe, Illinois. Reprinted with permission for worldwide and electronic rights.

usually enclosed in circles or boxes of some type, and indicate relationships between concepts with connecting lines. Words on the lines specify the relationships. The concepts are represented in a hierarchical order, from the most inclusive and general concepts at the top of the map to the most specific, less general concepts at the bottom. Teachers may encourage students to use color coding to group sections of the map. As they draw concept maps, students are engaged in meta-cognitive processes to resolve critical issues. They articulate a question or problem around which to build the map, and they figure out which is a central concept and how other concepts that they have previously learned are related to a new concept, topic, or problem.

For teachers, concept maps reflect the degree of clarity and relationships students project between their new and prior knowledge. Concept maps can help teachers assess prior knowledge and identify misconceptions, evaluate the quality of the students' learning, and identify areas of weakness in the development of conceptual links.

Reciprocal Instruction

Reciprocal Instruction, developed by Palincsar and Brown (1984, 1985), is perhaps the most studied instructional method for modeling meta-cognitive behaviors (Rosenshine & Meister, 1994). In this approach, meta-cognitive awareness develops in guided, small-group discussions following individual work on given assignments. In these group discussions, students learn to summarize, identify ambiguities, ask questions, and predict future learning. When this technique is applied to mathematics instruction, after all students complete a task, one student takes the lead in presenting his or her summary or conclusion of the assignment. If other students reached different conclusions, then the ensuing discussion would be articulated by key questions that help the group identify the confusing parts of the task, the different conceptual understandings, or the different procedures that have led the group to the various conclusions. At this point, the students may decide to ask a teacher to help, or the teacher may decide to ask the group a question or offer a clue that would render the group discussion more constructive. Finally, the group members must predict what the teacher would teach next.

5. Appropriate Communication

Whether oral or written, classroom communication is of critical importance to the learning process. Teachers and students benefit the most when they receive and interpret each other accurately (see Figure 3.10).

Clearly, there are several possibilities for classroom communication to fail. The teacher may fail to say what she means, the student may not hear or may fail to interpret what the teacher says as intended, the student may fail to say what he means, and the teacher may fail to hear or properly interpret what the student says. If any of these happen, the communication between the teacher and the student fails and detracts from the quality of learning. Therefore, while maintaining students' attention and active involvement, teachers must ensure that the communication does not depend on mathematical terms that are not well known to all students or may not be used correctly.

The formal verbal language of mathematics is significant for at least two reasons. First, it is significant because most of the verbal terms—such as *angle, area, slope, function, product, quotient, mode, factor, variable, tangent, polygon, prime number, per-*

Figure 3.10
Appropriate Communication

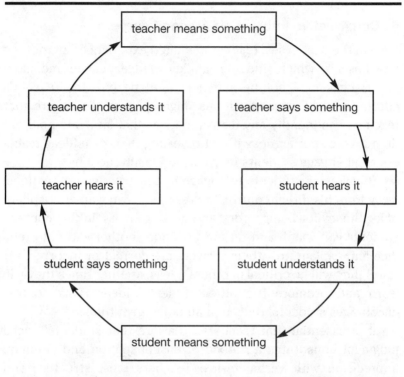

mutation, cosine, irrational number, and many others—function as "conceptual packages." Terms such as these do not represent particular objects. They are abstract categories that conceptually organize mathematics. Second, the verbal language is significant to mathematics simply because that language is the essential tool of dialogue about specific mathematical ideas—a tool of teaching and learning. Students who lack the formal language of mathematics have difficulties reasoning and communicating about mathematics. Therefore, the teacher will succeed best if she helps her students build the formal language that replaces their metaphoric, informal expressions.

In the learning process, the new tier of the students' vocabulary knowledge may coexist with the formal vocabulary of mathematics. To avoid student misconceptions while they learn to "pack" new concepts in the formal vocabulary of mathematics, teachers must try to understand the naive metaphoric language students use to communicate their reasoning.

6. Constructive Interaction Among Learners

Even in the best cases, teacher-mediated experiences are not the only basis by which students gain knowledge. Teacher-mediated experiences may not be sufficient, and despite the teacher's efforts, student misconceptions might persist. To ensure that teachers can identify any distorted ideas that students hold but do not voice nor argue, without revealing their own ideas teachers must engage students in constructive interactions.

By allowing students to engage in constructive interactions, away from his direct control, the teacher creates an atmosphere of legitimacy for being wrong and making errors. In this context, students can watch and reason with one another without prejudice and explain how their answers are correct or incorrect. At times they will be critical of others' ideas; at other times they will learn and promote the other students' ideas. This context encourages students' reflection and divergent thinking.

It is essential that teachers be aware that students' social judgment constitutes a hotbed of misconception and common imprecision with verbal terms. Teachers must structure and monitor students' arguments to ensure that students identify misconceptions. They must ensure that when students argue, misconceptions are not reinforced and students indeed make progress in their conceptual understanding. Teachers must intervene or regroup students to facilitate a constructive dialogue.

If it meets certain conditions, cooperative learning is an effective tool for promoting dialogues about misconceptions. These conditions include the following parameters:

- The dialogue challenges students to use higher-order thinking. When students compare, analyze, predict, and assess misconceptions, they are engaging in constructive dialogue.
- The interaction is constructive. The students, working together, learn to perceive themselves as a cooperative community of mathematical investigators.

- Each individual takes responsibility to engage his or her teammates in the dialogue. Each is more willing to share hypotheses and question the theories of others.

- The dialogue promotes reflective thinking among the team members. Alone and together, the students think about thinking.

- The dialogue promotes the development of social skills needed for constructive interaction. These include listening, clarifying, summarizing different points of view, and predicting.

Group work that fails to meet these parameters is unlikely to help students maintain focus and correct misconceptions.

Students modify their preconceptions and replace their faulty intuitions with mathematical concepts if and only if they are dissatisfied with them and find the mathematical concepts to be more plausible and more fruitful. Otherwise, if they cannot assimilate new experiences that conflict with their preconceptions and faulty intuitions, they "learn" to hold multiple and often contradictory ideas at the same time (Konold, 1989, 1991; Shaugnessy, 1993). Even when these students appear to have modified their beliefs as they provide correct answers on examinations and quizzes, in less formal situations they continue to operate according to their misconceptions (De Lisi & Golbeck, 1999).

Summary

Concept-Rich Instruction views the procedural knowledge and the conceptual knowledge of mathematics as interrelated. According to this view, it is worthwhile to distinguish between misconceptions that are learned in the classroom and preconceptions and false naive intuitions that students *bring with them to the classroom*. Because misconceptions result in systematic errors, reflective teachers can easily recognize misconceptions by analyzing errors.

Learning mathematical concepts reflects a transition from preconceptions to more-encompassing and better-defined concepts. The relative levels of conceptual understanding reflect a degree of flexibility and decontextualization. Undergeneralization is evident in limited understanding and limited application of concepts, and overgeneralization is reflected in the application of poorly understood concepts or rules where they are irrelevant or inappropriate. Intuition plays a role only with basic beliefs that are true by insistence, not by proof, and are referred to as mathematical axioms (postulates).

Teachers must treat misconceptions as psycho-logic conditions. Instruction that aims at altering misconceptions must be well informed about the cognitive structures underlying the related content and must be carefully executed. It generally features six parameters: reciprocity, flexibility, alternative representations of new concepts, meta-cognitive reflection, appropriate communication, and constructive interaction among students.

Knowing mathematic concepts implies a realization that the concepts can be applied to solving problems. However, solving problems mathematically depends not only on the knowledge of mathematic concepts, but also on a host of additional affective dispositions and cognitive and meta-cognitive abilities that define good thinking. A discussion of the affective dispositions and the cognitive and meta-cognitive abilities that are necessary for solving problems mathematically, and the related instructional implications, is now in good order.

Chapter 4

Solving Problems Mathematically

Many teachers agree that solving problems mathematically involves important cognitive dispositions and skills. The rhetoric of problem solving has been so pervasive among mathematics educators over the last two decades, however, that this agreement has taken on different interpretations, and the related arguments have become confused and misleading. First, many teachers do not distinguish between "doing exercises" and "solving problems." Second, many confuse the idea of structuring mathematics instruction around problem-solving activities with the idea of teaching the strategies of problem solving. Third, some view problem solving as a process or ability, while others view it as content knowledge.

Consider first the issue of doing exercises compared with solving problems. Exercises are typically considered to be tasks that challenge students to apply known procedures to similar situations. In contrast, problem solving requires analysis, heuristics, and reasoning toward self-defined goals (Smith, 1991). It is clear from this distinction that many students are mostly engaged in doing exercises. They are asked only to apply or match given procedures to similar "problems." True problem-solving activities are rare in most mathematics lessons. If students are to learn how to solve problems, teachers must engage them with real problems on a regular basis.

Second, solving problems is not just a means for finding correct answers. Rather, it is a vehicle for developing logical thinking; it provides a context for mathematics and an opportunity for the transfer of newly acquired concepts and ideas. To the degree that problems simulate real life, solving them endows mathematics with meaning. Unfortunately, solving word problems is one of the least popular and least addressed aspects of the mathematics curriculum among students and teachers.

Regarding the third issue, which distinguishes problem solving as process from problem solving as content, abundant research indicates that competent problem solvers can recall the mathematical essence of problems much better than their contexts. Weaker students tend to recall the contexts, but not the essence of the problems (Carpenter, Fennema, Peterson, Chiang, & Loef, 1989).

The lesson from this research divides mathematics teachers into two camps. One camp of teachers has been quick to take the shortcut of seeking to automate students' problem solving through the teaching of "key words," algorithms, and other tricks that work for given types of problems. This approach shelters students from the uncertain nature of problem solving. The other camp of teachers seeks ways to enhance the efficacy of reflective practices and of student-generated activities, thus provoking and surprising students through cognitive dissonance.

The first camp of teachers, particularly among algebra teachers, has taken the position that symbolic equation solving and routine computations should precede word problem solving because computing tasks are easier for students (Nathan & Koedinger, 2000). Most textbook publishers reinforce this perception by their practice of placing word problems at the end of chapters. On the other hand, the second camp of teachers understands that the most important idea of algebra is exactly that of modeling real situations (Nathan & Koedinger, 2000). They realize that knowing how to manipulate algebraic equations, use graphs, and understand functions is useless unless this knowledge is applicable to solving problems. They have opted to teach symbolic equation solving in tandem with word problem solving.

Teaching Word Problems: An Instructional Challenge

There is a discrepancy between the good intelligence of many students and their dismal performance in some areas of mathematics. Solving word problems in mathematics belongs in this paradox. The explanation has much to do with the way teachers teach and students learn. Despite the research, many teachers cling to the misconception that students fail to solve word problems because they lack the mathematical aptitude. This misconception offers false justification for the perpetual poor statistics of student achievement. Many teachers keep teaching mathematics the way they were taught and are reluctant to adopt even the most successful instructional strategies that other subject-matter teachers have found effective (Lochhead & Zietsman, 2001).

One can find in the constructivist approach some of the conditions for effectively teaching how to solve problems mathematically:

- Elicit discussions around students' ideas and beliefs about the topic (problem) under consideration (Hewson & Thorley, 1989).
- Make provisions for learners to be able to clarify their ideas or beliefs through small-group work.
- Promote meta-cognitive discourse among the students to illuminate the nature of students' internal representations (Baird, Fensham, Gustone, & White, 1991; Beeth, 1993).
- Ensure that there will be direct contrast between learners' views and the desired canonical view (Hewson & Hewson, 1989).
- Employ "bridging analogies" (Clement, 1993).
- Provide immediate opportunities for learners to apply their newly acquired understanding to different examples (Hewson & Hewson, 1989) or phenomena of their own

interest, so that they can develop complex problem-posing and problem-solving skills (Jungck & Calley, 1985).

- Provide time to discuss the nature of learning (problem solving).

These strategies alone can alter mathematics lessons remarkably by bringing problem solving to the forefront and, at the same time, correcting the typical student's misconceptions of the discipline, such as the following (Cook, 2001):

- Mathematics is essentially computation.
- The important outcome in mathematics is the right answer.
- Mathematics problems have only one right answer.
- There is only one right way to solve a problem.
- The teacher and the textbook should not be questioned.

A concern with student misconceptions of mathematics motivated the current national debate on the severely untapped potential value of problem solving in the mathematics curriculum. Indeed, the most innovative idea in the standards of the National Council of Teachers of Mathematics (NCTM) is that problem solving ought to constitute a vehicle for the construction, evaluation, and refinement of students' own theories about mathematics, and the development of their confidence in their own ability to think mathematically. Teaching problem solving must certainly be examined from this perspective. Teachers must consider problem solving not only as an end, but as a means of instruction.

Problem Solving as Instructional Means

Some teachers argue against problem-based mathematics instruction. They postulate that

- Problem solving is too difficult for many students.
- Problem solving takes too much time (not enough time in the curriculum for problem solving).
- Problem solving is not tested on proficiency tests.
- Before they can solve problems, students must master facts, procedures, and algorithms.

- Appropriate mathematics problems are not readily available.
- Problem solving is not in the textbook.

Comparisons of instructional practices by their effect on student achievement do not fare well with such arguments. Indeed, such comparisons show exactly the contrary. For example, the Third International Mathematics and Science Study indicates that students achieve more when learning is based on problem solving rather than on recall-based instruction (Wilson & Blank, 1999). Like many other studies, the TIMSS study shows that mathematics lessons based on solving new and interesting problems can be more effective and efficient than lessons based on memorization. According to this study, instruction centered on problem solving gets better results with all students, including those low-performing groups identified in the No Child Left Behind Act (special education, English as a second language, and low socioeconomic groups).

Mathematicians who maintain that problem solving is the heart of mathematics also take the position that mathematics instruction is best organized as a set of problem-solving experiences. Experts in the psychology of learning and in mathematics education point to additional learning advantages of problem-based instruction, or a constructive approach, particularly in the area of mathematics. Among these advantages are the following:

- Promotion of active involvement.
- Facilitation of intrinsic motivation, excitement, and challenge in place of boredom.
- Development of meaning.
- Engagement in purposeful learning.
- Promotion of greater concentration and persistence; increased time on task.
- Direct practice with mathematical concepts before symbols and recording.
- Engagement of thinking.
- Facilitation of repetition without tedium.
- Encouragement of self-regulation and monitoring.

- Perception that all students believe they have an equal likelihood of success.

- Inherent enjoyment and success that foster positive attitudes about the self and mathematics.

- Stimulation of creativity and imagination and encouragement of cooperative learning.

- Stimulation of classroom dialogue, communication, and the development of interpersonal skills.

Thus a teacher of mathematics has a great opportunity. If he fills his allotted time with drilling his students in routine operations, he kills their interest, hampers their intellectual development, and misuses his opportunity. But if he challenges the curiosity of his students by setting them problems proportionate to their knowledge, and helps them to solve their problems with stimulating questions, he may give them a taste for, and some means of, independent thinking (Pólya, 1945, p. V).

How Is This Notion Applied?

Consider, for example, introducing students to the geometrical concepts of perimeter and area as described in the following classroom scenario.

The class had not been previously introduced to the term "perimeter" and had little exposure to the term "area." Students were instructed to work in pairs and were allowed to move around in the classroom. The teacher presented the class with the following problem:

> Suppose one had 100 yards of fencing. What shapes of gardens could be fenced? What are the dimensions of each shape (draw)? What is the area of each shape?

The teacher intervened only when students had questions. She encouraged the students to look up the words "dimensions" and "area" in the dictionary on their own. All students were fully engaged in the activity.

In 35 minutes, all were able to think about, and figure out correctly, the area of a square with a perimeter of 100 feet. About one-third of the students realized that rectangular gardens of the same perimeter could have different dimensions and different areas.

For the last five minutes of the lesson, the class regrouped and, in answering the teacher's questions, students defined the relevant geometrical terms and wrote their definitions on the board (including the related computational procedures). For homework, students were asked to draw five rectangular garden shapes of the same perimeter (100 feet) and compute the area of each.

It is easy to imagine why students in this class would know the geometrical concepts better than students who just memorized facts; why they will do better on proficiency tests; how such lessons do not consume more time than other types of lessons. Learning is stimulated by a need to solve an interesting problem, and it culminates with new insights about mathematics.

> Good problems can introduce students to fundamental ideas and to the importance of mathematical reasoning and proof. Good problems can serve as starting points for serious explorations and generalizations. Their solutions can motivate students to value the processes of mathematical modeling and abstraction and develop students' competence with the tools and logic of mathematics. (Schoenfeld, 1994)

Finding interesting mathematics problems is easier than it has ever been with the help of recently published textbooks and the great number of instructional Web sites. Most teachers already know this.

Problem Solving as Instructional Ends

It is also true that many teachers are concerned that for reasons of poor cognitive and meta-cognitive dispositions, or because of poor motivation, some students approach mathematics word problems aimlessly, randomly, and unsystematically. If these teachers are right, then students who perform poorly need to learn how to process mathematics word problems. They need instruction that targets the processes of problem solving they fail to do efficiently. This instruction is too often absent.

> All too often we focus on a narrow collection of well-defined tasks and train students to execute those tasks in a routine, if not algorithmic fashion. Then we test the students on tasks that are very close to the ones they have been taught. If they succeed on those problems, we and they congratulate each other on the fact that they have learned some powerful mathematical techniques. In fact,

they may be able to use such techniques mechanically while lacking some rudimentary thinking skills. To allow them, and ourselves, to believe that they "understand" the mathematics is deceptive and fraudulent. (Schoenfeld, 1988)

Most teachers are aware of some of the obvious, but not all the important, factors that determine the difficulty of solving word problems. Teachers must consider the critical role of prerequisite mathematics knowledge (concepts and operations), and often must consider the language requirements and the level of complexity of the problems (number of steps or amount of information to be considered). With word problems, however, teachers often fail to consider the more subtle cognitive and meta-cognitive functions that discriminate between successful and failing attempts at solutions. The balance of this chapter will analyze these cognitive and meta-cognitive functions.

Solving Word Problems: A Cognitive Challenge

Failure to solve problems mathematically may or may not be the result of poor understanding of the underlying mathematical concepts. Students may fail to solve problems because they misunderstand the underlying mathematical concepts, or they may fail despite their good conceptual understanding of the necessary mathematical concepts. For example, almost all 5-year-olds know how they should count. Namely, they know that they need to assign only one number word to every counted object. Their errors in counting are the result of either skipping or counting an object twice. These are errors of execution rather than misconception.

To solve problems successfully, students must rely upon mathematical concepts and an integrated and functional grasp of a hierarchy of mathematical concepts that connect different areas (Bransford, Brown, & Cocking, 1999; Carpenter & Lehrer, 1999). At the same time, they must apply strategic competence: They must define the problem, select relevant information, formulate and represent that information, plan and then modify the process as needed, and verify that their strategy works (Mayer & Wittrock, 1996; Schoenfeld, 1992). Ultimately, able problem solvers construct, translate, evaluate, and refine theories about mathematics by creating, conjecturing, exploring, testing, and verifying them (Lester et al., 1994). Although misconceptions result in systematic errors, lack of strategic competence appears in unsystematic errors.

Teachers know that some errors in problem solving appear to be unsystematic. They know that even students with solid conceptual mathematical understanding may stumble as they attempt to solve problems and resort to guesswork. With better understanding, teachers can target strategic competencies effectively. Even informed teachers, however, may wonder how their own understanding of the strategic competencies of problem solving can help them analyze students' unsystematic errors. They are particularly puzzled because they correctly infer from their experiences with problem solving that

- There could be different erroneous outcomes from a failed attempt to solve problems.
- Apparently similar errors may have different causes.
- Any error may result from a confluence of processing problems.
- A student who fails to solve a problem at one time may solve it (or similar problems) successfully at other times.

Indeed, errors in problem solving that do not emanate from misconceptions often appear to be sloppy and inconsistent. However, when the processes that lead to errors are assessed, the reasons often appear systematic. Research in mathematics education provides some insights into the problems in the processing of mathematical problems. This research indicates problems in imaging, formal logical operations, memory, and language skills. Although teachers must understand strategic competency and know effective instructional strategies that facilitate their development, teachers must also learn how to analyze students' errors in the *processes* of problem solving.

- Some students who fail to solve problems have difficulties translating the context of problems into mathematical symbol systems because they lack imaging strategies. These students do not draw diagrams because they are unable to produce useful images (Novak, 1990). This difficulty is apparent if teachers observe the student at work. Where it exists, it is consistent, at least with the type of problems for which the solution relies upon imaging strategies. Consider, for example, students trying to solve the calendar problem:

> If the fifth day of a given month is a Tuesday, what is the date of the last Friday of the same month?

When we presented this problem individually to 4th-grade students, we found that only about 40 percent of them drew a calendar as a means to help them think the solution through. The others treated the problem as a numerical arithmetical problem or as a counting problem (counting days and dates coordinately).

The difficulty of translating the context of problems into mathematical symbol systems because of poor imaging strategies is common in student errors across different areas of mathematics. Solving arithmetic story problems may require imaging such as in the example above; the solution to algebra problems may involve graphing and organizing given data in schemas of different sorts; many geometry problems can be solved only if they are properly translated from verbal statements to drawings; probability and statistics problems involve mapping tree diagrams and drawing different kinds of graphs that feature event outcomes or organize data; and trigonometry problems always require translation across verbal, symbolic, and visual representation. Although some imaging can be done in the mind and need not be featured in students' drawings and diagrams—as is certainly the case with some students who successfully solve mathematics problems—if teachers insist on seeing the students' work, they will gain access to students' visual imaging. Compared with teachers in other disciplines, mathematics teachers can most easily identify poor imaging strategies when it is the case for students who struggle to solve problems.

- Cognitive research in mathematics also indicates that failure at problem solving is related to poor logical operational abilities (Campbell, Collis, & Watson, 1993, 1995). The failure to solve problems may be inherent in students' failure to form hypotheses and check them out, searching for negative evidence and attending to inconvenient facts, or posing questions without knowing whether answers or new methods that will lead to solutions exist. It is also inherent in student difficulties with formal logical operations, such as those involved in analogical thinking, deduction, and induction. As will be discussed later, poor logical operational abilities are always featured in the processes that lead to errors, not in the errors themselves.

- The working memory of some students who have difficulties solving arithmetic problems is incapable of holding the original problem in mind while processing different parts of the solution (Koontz & Berch, 1996). Research in mathematical disabilities, as defined by poor standardized test scores (Geary, 1994), and research with "not-so-good" mathematics students indicate deficiency in the retrieval of backup strategies (Siegler, 2003).

From a broader perspective of cognitive research, psychologists have classified processing problems in terms of inefficient input or gathering of information, elaboration or processing, and output or communication. For example, Reuven Feuerstein identifies 29 functions and classifies them in terms of these three phases, as shown in figure 4.1 (Feuerstein & Rand, 1997). Deficiencies in these functions can be very consistent in a student's operations, even if they produce what appears as unsystematic errors.

The basic framework for most research on mathematics problem solving in the past three decades can be traced to the writings of George Pólya. He identified several components of the process of problem solving and the relationships among them. These components describe the process as much more flexible than the "steps of problem solving" that are often delineated in textbooks. One of the misunderstandings of Pólya's research is

Figure 4.1

Cognitive Functions

Impaired Cognitive Functions at the Input Level:
- Blurred and sweeping perception.
- Unplanned, impulsive, and unsystematic exploratory behavior.
- Lack of or impaired receptive verbal tools that affect discrimination (e.g., objects, events, and relationships are inappropriately labeled).
- Lack of or impaired spatial orientation and lack of stable terms of reference by which to establish topological and Euclidian organization of space.
- Lack of or impaired temporal concepts.
- Lack of or impaired conservation of constancies (e.g., size, shape, quantity, color, orientation) across variations in one or more dimensions.
- Lack of or deficient need for precision and accuracy in data gathering.
- Lack of capacity to consider two or more sources of information at once. This is reflected in dealing with data in a piecemeal fashion rather than as a unit of organized facts.

Impaired Cognitive Functions at the Elaboration Level:
- Inadequate perception of the existence of a problem and its definition.
- Inability to select relevant, as opposed to irrelevant, cues in defining a problem.
- Lack of spontaneous comparative behavior or the limitation of its application to a restricted need system.
- Narrowness of the mental field.
- Episodic grasp of reality.
- Lack of need for the eduction or establishment of relationships.
- Lack of need for or exercise of summative behavior.
- Lack of or impaired need for pursing logical evidence.
- Lack of or impaired inferential hypothetical ("if . . . then") thinking.
- Lack of or impaired strategies for hypothesis testing.
- Lack of or impaired planning behavior.
- Lack of or impaired interiorization.
- Nonelaboration of certain cognitive categories because the verbal concepts are not part of the individual's verbal inventory on a receptive level, or because they are not mobilized at the expressive level.

Impaired Cognitive Functions at the Output Level:
- Egocentric comm
- Impulsive, randunication modalities.
- Difficulty in projecting virtual relationships.
- Blocking.
- Trial-and-error responses.
- Lack of or impaired verbal or other tools for communicating adequately elaborated responses.
- Lack of or impaired need for precision and accuracy in communicating responses.
- Deficiency of visual transport.
- Impulsive, random, unplanned behavior.

From *Dynamic Assessment of Cognitive Modifiability*, by Reuven Feuerstien, Yaacov Rand, Rafi Feuerstein, and Lou Falik, copyright by ICELP Press, Jerusalem, Israel, (2002). Reprinted with permission for worldwide and electronic rights.

that the process is linear and that it can simply be memorized, practiced, and habituated. In fact, at any point in the process the solver may reexamine the given data, change the data back and forth across different representations, shift strategies, and correct a solution more than once. To understand Pólya's position, it is important to examine the components of the problem-solving process that he identified:

- Understanding the problem and identifying a target goal;
- Translating verbal and other information into the mathematical language without changing the meaning;
- Planning a solution;
- Solving the problem; and
- Reviewing and evaluating the solution in the context of the problem.

Figure 4.2 illustrates the relations among these components.

Figure 4.2
The Problem-Solving Process

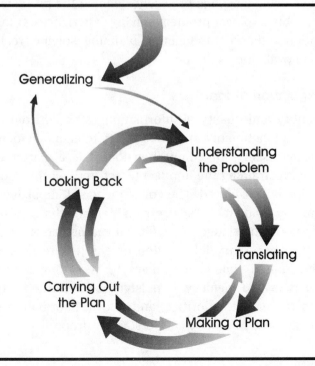

Pólya's components of problem solving describe cognitive and meta-cognitive operations. A teacher who understands not only the meta-cognitive operations but also the cognitive processes underlying these components can find consistency in errors that appear at times as unsystematic, and intervene effectively when it is necessary to modify the student's work on problems.

As the balance of this chapter will show, Pólya's components of problem solving and Feuerstein's cognitive functions can together provide a helpful didactic tool in the hands of mathematics teachers and a constructive tool of analysis of errors in problem solving.

Understanding the Problem

Solving word problems involves understanding what is given and what is expected. Yet, the processes that determine the quality and quantity of the information that is gathered from a verbal statement of the problem could be more complex than they appear to be. These processes challenge a wide range of cognitive, meta-cognitive, and linguistic dispositions, including self-regulating, using language precisely, defining the problem, relating the problem to past problem-solving experiences, translating information in different modalities, planning, solving (realizing a plan), and evaluating solutions.

Self-Regulation of Input

The quantity and quality of information gathered from a word problem is a function of a student's ability to maintain focus over the time necessary for comprehension. It is a matter of self-regulation: restraining the impulse to act until all the necessary information is considered. The consequence of impulsive action is commonly evident in "silly errors," errors that are not the result of poor knowledge or inefficient mathematics skills. The omission of necessary information or careless reading results from the limited time commitment to recording information before it is lost to memory. Impulsivity also detracts from the ability to reorganize, prioritize, and reform information that is actually gathered in order to understand it properly.

Think about the time needed to read, reorganize, prioritize, and reform this problem statement until you understand it: Fifty gallons of liquid were poured into two containers of different size. Express the amount of liquid poured into the larger container in terms of the amount poured into the smaller container.

The relationship between the typical classroom culture and self-regulation is often antagonistic. Many teachers ask questions and do not wait long enough for all students to think before they respond; teachers often use timed tests; students often compete against each other to voice the first responses to questions. Impulsive behavior is, in fact, encouraged and reinforced by this culture. To modify it, teachers must start by altering the culture. Students should be credited for careful reading and full understanding of word problems and discouraged from premature attempts to solve problems or offering irrelevant responses to questions. Students should be guided and asked to reflect about the nature of their analysis using questions such as the following:

- Was it easy to understand?
- Why?
- What did you have to do before you could understand?
- How?

Teachers should understand that impulsive, unregulated behaviors are habitual. To alter these bad habits means replacing them with newly established habits of reflective behavior.

Precise Use of Language

All word problems involve decoding information about relationships and operations among known and unknown quantities. The words used to convey such information are often referred to as "key" words (see Figure 4.3).

The wording of mathematics problems is not always "user friendly," and given relationships—even available facts—may have to be reformed before they can be used in mathematical expressions.

Figure 4.3
Key Words

Addition		
increased by	total of	together
more than	combined	sum
added to		

Subtraction		
decreased by	minus	more than
difference between/of	less than	
fewer than		

Multiplication		
of	times	product of
increased by	decreased by	multiplied by
a factor of		

Division		
per	quotient of	out of
a ratio of	percent	

Relations		
is, are, was, were, will be	gives	
yields	sold for	

A student may have to replace referents by their reciprocals (e.g., A $\Rightarrow$ B revised to B $\Leftarrow$ A; see Figure 4.4) and revise quantities as a result of incompatible units of measurement.

Because key words represent mathematical ideas, knowledge of them is a matter of particular concern for students who are not native English speakers. Teachers should know that all students, including bilingual students, acquire important terms more effectively through sheltered instruction—in the context of genuine classroom dialogues about content (Achevarria & Graves, 1998). Teachers have to be careful not to put too much emphasis on teaching key words out of context, because students may cling to the surface feature of key words without understanding the mathematical ideas. Research has shown that such students fail to solve word problems, particularly where word problems involve key words that are not relevant (Carpenter, 1989).

Figure 4.4
Translation of Verbal Information on Relationships to Mathematical Codes

Verbal expression	Mathematical expression
1. "3 less than X"	"X – 3"
2. "the difference of X and y"	"X – y," not "y – X"
3. "X multiplied by 5"	"5 • X"
4. "the quotient of X and y"	$\dfrac{X}{y}$
5. "the ratio of X and y"	$\dfrac{X}{y}$
6. "the ratio of 3 more than X to X"	$\dfrac{(X + 3)}{X}$
7. "five less than the total of a number and three"	"(y + 3) – 5"

Note: In the cases numbered 1, 3, 6, and 7, the information must be reformed in the process of translation into mathematical expressions.

There are also verbal terms that do not explicitly indicate the relationships among known and unknown quantities. The terms used in the word problem imply the relationships. Such terms as the geometry concepts of volume and area, mechanical physics concepts of speed (rate) and pressure, and financial concepts of interest and exchange rate imply certain relationships and operations; their use in word problems requires knowledge of such implications.

Examples of mathematical relationships that are implicit include the following:

1. Which is faster, a car that travels a distance of 50 miles in 1.5 hours or one that travels 70 miles in 2 hours?

2. What is the area of the equilateral triangle that is enclosed by a circle with a 2" diameter?

Teachers should consider the language of word problems as a matter of necessary knowledge and always ensure that students can infer the needed relationships before they are asked to solve word problems.

Relating a Problem to
Past Problem-Solving Experiences

Problem solving in mathematics also requires a well-organized base of nonverbal conceptual knowledge. Research shows that successful problem solvers categorize math problems on the basis of their mathematical structure (Schoenfeld & Herrmann, 1982; Silver, 1979). For example, in working with trigonometric identities (high school curriculum), successful solvers always convert all expressions to functions of sine and cosine and then simplify. Past experiences are critical. More important, however, teachers must understand how the organization of past experiences influences students' new attempts to solve problems.

New problems must always trigger comparative processes by which they can be accommodated in larger schemata of problem types. These comparative processes are operated by analogies and constitute a powerful learning mechanism. The principle that underlies all analogies is the following:

As A is to (in) B, so C is to (in) D

Familiar   New

The fruitfulness of analogies depends on whether the resemblance between the new and the familiar is fundamental or merely of a precarious, superficial nature. Analogies can be based on the resemblance in context or in the resemblance of function. In mathematics word problems, contextual analogies are limited to superficial features, and functional analogies are based on the mathematical operations and schemata. Let us examine the two types carefully.

Analogies by Context

Students commonly draw analogies among mathematics word problems in terms of context (see Figure 4.5). They assume that the problem's context discriminates among methods of solution, levels of difficulty, or types of operations. Research flatly refutes this assumption (Nesher & Hershkovitz, 1994; Silver, 1994). For example, recognizing a problem as a "coin problem" or as a "rate/distance/speed problem" does not at all determine the abil-

Figure 4.5

Typical Categories of Classification
for Algebraic Word Problems, by Context

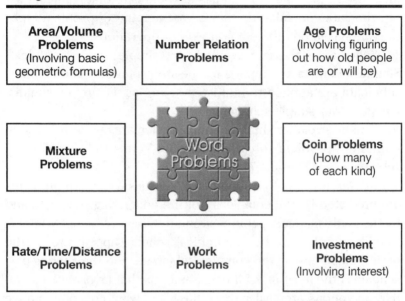

ity to solve it. Research shows that reliance on these features is predominant among low-performing students. The common contextual feature that is worthy of consideration is the use of common concepts with terms such as speed, area, or pressure.

Functional analogies are more fundamental and directly connected to the mathematical structure. Such analogies characterize the way expert problem solvers develop their models of problem types. Unfortunately, such analogies often remain tacit and absent in the classroom dialogue.

Analogies by Functional Schemata

Studies in the solving of word problems conclude that effective analogies primarily elaborate semantic structures, and secondarily the mathematical operations involved (Nesher & Hershkovitz, 1994). As they read the verbal text, successful problem solvers first identify the semantic structure and then comprehend the entire semantic set relations on the basis of past experiences (Nesher & Hershkovitz, 1994). Only when the analogous schemata are established are successful solvers prepared to focus on the specific operations and the computation they must use in the solution. Studies also indicate that a smaller set of schemata can substitute for a vast amount of problem types that are based on different contexts or operations.

Schemata can be classified as "simple" and "complex." Simple schemata are applied to one-step solutions, and complex schemata are applied to multistep solutions. Figure 4.6 summarizes the four simple schemata.

The interrelationships of simple schemata, as in the case of multistep problem-solving processes, constitute "complex" schemata (see Figure 4.7).

Research shows that students' difficulties with word problems are predicted by the complexity of the underlying schemata and by the mathematical operations required to solve them (Nesher & Hershkovitz, 1994). The hierarchical scheme appears to be the least difficult among the complex schemata, and the sharing-part scheme is the most difficult one. Solutions that involve commutative operations are easier than those involving noncommutative operations. The order of difficulty in terms of the basic mathematic operations, from the easiest to the hardest, is multiplication ($\cdot$),

Figure 4.6
Simple Schemata in Solving One-Step Word Problems

Join	Unknown result add/multiply (altogether)	Change unknown subtract/divide (missing)	Start unknown add/multiply (more, less)
Separate	Unknown subtract/divide (left, remainder)	Change unknown subtract/divide (left over)	Start unknown subtract/divide
Relate (part-whole)	Whole known add/multiply (altogether)		Part unknown subtract/divide
Compare	Difference unknown subtract/divide (more, less)	Compare quantities add/multiply (more, less)	Referent unknown Add/multiply subtract/divide (more, less)

Figure 4.7

Complex Schemata in Solving Two-Step Word Problems

	Scheme	Structural Relationship	Example	Model
L E V E L O F D I F F I C U L T Y	*Hierarchical*	The whole of one structure is part* of the other structure.	A total of 35 flowers are distributed equally among 7 vases. Each vase has 2 roses and the rest are tulips. How many tulips are there in each vase?	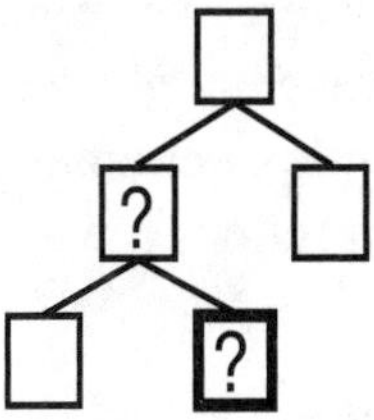
	Sharing Whole	The two structures share* one whole.	There are 20 boys and 12 girls in the camp. They are divided into 4 equal groups. How many children are there in each group?	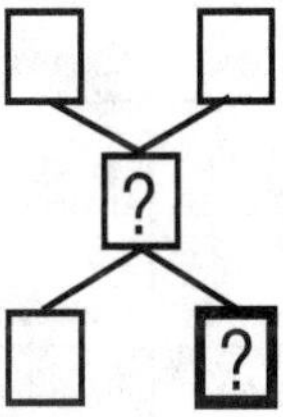
	Sharing Part	The two structures share* one part.	At the party there were 20 children, 12 of whom were boys. The 40 flowers that were left from the party were distributed equally among the girls. How many flowers did each girl get?	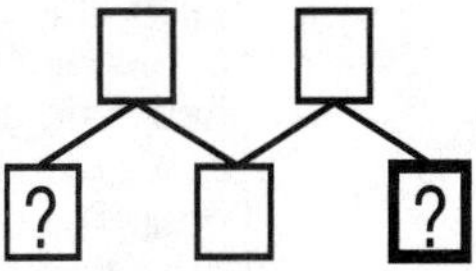

*The relationships are represented in terms of the four operations.

addition (+), division (/), and subtraction (−) (Carpenter, Fennema, Franke, Empson, & Levy, 1999; Nesher & Hershkovitz, 1994).

Solving interesting word problems is best followed by classroom dialogues. In these dialogues teachers should lead students to reflect upon the solution process and generalize the nature of relationships between the known and unknown components and the structure of these relationships that make the scheme. These dialogues should lead students to generalize the four basic and three complex schemata so that the students can use them later as the organizing themes of analogies among problem-solving experiences. The contextual features should always be secondary in the instructional considerations.

Even in the limited examples in Figure 4.8, eight problems represent eight types of contexts, but only three simple and three complex schemata, or 7/8 of all the fundamental schemata that researchers have identified.

Figure 4.8

Problems by Common Contextual Categories
Analyzed by Relationships and Schemata

Context	Example	Relationship	Schemata
Number problems	A number is 3 less than 3 times another number. Their sum is 57. What are the numbers?	Explicit less than, times, sum of	Simple: compare $x = y - 3$ Complex: hierarchical $x + y = 57$
Distance problems	Two trains leave Washington, D.C., and New York at the same time and move toward each other. One train is moving at a speed of 40 miles per hour, and the other is moving at a speed of 60 miles per hour. The distance between the cities is 250 miles. At the same time, a fly is moving back and forth between the trains at a speed of 120 miles per hour. How many miles will the fly travel until the trains meet?	Implicit: $d = rt$	Simple: Join $40x + 60x = 250$ Complex: Sharing part $120x$
Mixture problems	A solution containing 5% salt is to be mixed with 3 ounces of a solution containing 10% salt to obtain a solution with 8% salt. How much of the first solution must be used?	Explicit: mixed with Implicit: %	Simple: Relate part/whole $5/100x$, $3(10/100)$, $(x + 3)(8/100)$ Complex: Sharing part $5/100x + 3(10/100) = (x + 3)(8/100)$
Area problems	The hypotenuse of a right triangle is 2 feet longer than the shorter leg. The longer leg is 1 foot more than the other leg. Find the lengths of the three sides.	Explicit: longer than, shorter than, more than Implicit: $l_1^2 + l_2^2 = h^2$	Simple: Compare x, $(x + 1)$, $(x + 2)$

continued

Defining the Problem

Even where word problems are followed by question marks, defining a problem is not a matter of simple reading. Rather, a problem definition must arise in the students' minds once they sort out the given and unknown information and the relationships among them. Because the problem definition endows the solution process with awareness and clear goals, absence of the need or the ability to define the problem is most likely to result in failing attempts to solve word problems. Research on the way students approach word problems reveals a significant deficiency of both—need and ability.

Figure 4.8, continued

Context	Example	Relationship	Schemata
Age problems	Jim is 4 years older than Linda. Their combined age is 20 years. How old is Jim and how old is Linda?	Explicit: older than, combined	Simple: Compare $j = l + 4$ Complex: Hierarchical $j + l + 4 = 20$
Work problems	Joe can paint a house in 8 hours. It takes Jim 5 hours to paint the same house. How long will it take both to paint the house if they work together?	Explicit: together Implicit: work rate	Simple: Join Complex: Sharing whole $1/8x + 8x = 40$
Percent problems	Madeleine Jones invested $10,000. Part of this amount she saved in a bank account at 5% interest per year, and the rest in bonds that yield a 7% annual return. How much was each investment, if the annual combined interest was $600?	Explicit: combined Implicit: % interest, return, yield	Simple: part/whole relationships Complex: Sharing whole $5/100x + 7/100 (10,000 - x) = 600$
Coin problems	A jar contains quarters, dimes, and nickels with a combined value of $3.95. If there are twice as many quarters as dimes, and one less nickel than dimes, how many coins of each kind are there?	Explicit*: combined, twice as many as, less than	Simple: Join Complex: Hierarchical $(0.25)2x + (0.10)x + (0.05)(x - 1) = 3.95$

*Students must also know the value of nickels, quarters, and dimes.

Many students process word problems without a logically determined procedure. This behavior is very common in the way primary school students solve problems in general (Piaget, 1995). It may also be true of many middle school students. The fact that this behavior "lingers on" with some high school students who are fully capable of acting logically outside the mathematics context, with full awareness and retrospection, shows that their failing operation with word problems is not a function of true cognitive ability. It may well be, again, a product of the common classroom culture.

Students perceive the act of asking questions of the teacher in the classroom as an indicator of ignorance that should be hidden (Dillon, 1988; Grasser & McMahen, 1993). They do not reflect upon what they do not know and usually ask questions only for which the answers are explicitly mentioned in the text (Grasser & Person, 1994; Mevarech & Susak, 1993). Consequently, even when students attempt to solve word problems, they take the definition that is literally provided without any attempt to interpret it and work aimlessly toward "correct answers." Teaching students to define problems well before they attempt to solve them may be the most important component of inquiry-based learning and the first ingredient of an assessment of student understanding (Silver & Cai, 1993). The quality of solution attempts can always be determined by students' ability to distinguish between clear and unclear problem definitions.

Studies have shown that when the questions posed at the end are removed from word problems, students' distinction between relevant and acceptable questions predict their success with problem solving. In other words, the questions that normally appear at the end of word problems may offer students yet another surface feature that masks the learning of processes and information necessary for students to define problems before students attempt to solve them, and ultimately clouds their sense of confidence in the solutions. Students learn to respond to the clues in the questions posed at the end of word problems, rather than trying to find the "problem" in the problem.

The Archimedes series, an innovative mathematics computer program, provides an example. It presents students with mathematics word problems from which the questions are eliminated, encouraging students to come up with the most relevant questions linked to the given information. According to the developers, the program is indeed effective in fostering students' awareness; flexibility; and logical, systematic, analytical thinking. The result should not be surprising. The definition of a problem determines the framework for the solution, which information is relevant and which information is not, and what are acceptable solutions (e.g., rough estimations, a choice of output form). Students who do not define problems are easily confused by extraneous information, cannot envision solutions, and therefore are likely to fail (Cawley, Fitzmaurice-Hayes, & Shaw, 1988).

Defining a problem may involve rephrasing an existing problem statement, defining a prerequisite problem before the stated one can be attempted, or identifying a solvable problem. Figure 4.9 illustrates these variations.

Figure 4.9

Variations in Problem Definitions

Example	Nature of Problem Definition	Outcome
There are13 boys and 16 girls in the group. How many children are there in the group?	Rephrasing the given definition (children vs. boys/girls)	What is the number of boys and girls together?
At the party there were 20 children, 12 of whom were boys. The 40 flowers that were left from the party were distributed equally among the girls. How many flowers did each girl get?	Implying a problem definition that must be solved before the explicitly stated one can be attempted.	How many girls were at the party?
Blue pencils cost 5¢ each and red pencils cost 6¢ each. Danny buys some blue and some red pencils and it altogether costs 90¢. If x is the number of blue pencils he bought, and y is the number of red pencils he bought, what can you write about x and y?	Identifying a problem where the problem definition is absent	How can the relationships among the given quantities be expressed in an algebraic equation form?

As Figure 4.9 indicates, rephrasing the definition of problems is not necessarily a simple matter of translation ("boys and girls" to "children"). It may involve the introduction of terms that are absent in the given word problem, including references to operations such as "together," "ratio," and "difference," and it must rely upon all explicit and implicit information.

The final goal of complex word problems may be readily defined in the given wording of problems. Because the solutions of such problems involve several steps, however, each of the steps constitutes simple subproblems that must be defined. Furthermore, because the subproblems are consequential, their definitions are subjects of priority. In the absence of given definitions, students must define the subproblems; they must consider the relevant set of available information and the missing information for each subproblem; and they must prioritize the subproblem definitions as a function of strategic reasoning and anticipation.

When the final goal is not defined in the word problem—sometimes referred to as an ill-structured or open-ended problem—the definition is entirely the function of the solvers. In this case, the solver must determine what missing information can possibly be deduced from the given information and judge whether it is worthy of a problem definition. Both the deduction and the judgment are matters of context and conceptual knowledge; and where there are alternatives, it may also be a matter of student perceptions set by teacher expectations and modeling, interest, and motivation.

Translating Word Problems into Mathematical Equations, Graphs, or Diagrams

It is well-documented that 4th grade students have difficulties comprehending arithmetic word problems. Although 73 percent of them can perform the basic operations with two- and three-digit numbers, only 33 percent can solve word problems involving these operations (National Assessment of Educational Progress [NAEP], 1996; see Liver, Alacaci, & Stylianou, 2000). Students at these grades cannot even retell the story problem in their own words. Reports indicate that solving algebraic word problems is also difficult for most 7th to 9th grade students. For most of these student, the difficulty has to do with the translation from one symbolic system (verbal-numeric-graphic) to another (diagram-letters-syntax). These translations constitute a real cognitive challenge.

As with all mathematics modeling of real-life situations, the cognitive challenge with word problems involves thinking and reasoning with variable representations and moving from one to the other efficiently. It is important that arithmetic students learn to draw a picture that illustrates a word problem before they attempt the solution, algebra students decide how to label variables with what they stand for, geometry students construct forms and divide them in different ways as they attempt a proof, and probability students draw a tree diagram to determine a sample space before they calculate event probabilities. Most important, students may all do that differently because there are different ways to draw pictures, label variables, construct forms, and draw diagrams. There may be as many variations of representation among students in one classroom as the number of students. What is common among them is that they are all "internal representations" that seek to transcend the limits of the worded statement, while maintaining compatibility with the external presentation. Consider, for example, the three entirely different representations that are possible with the problem in Figure 4.10.

The first difficulty of translation and modeling is rooted in the type of information that is available in word problems. It is often said that a student's solutions of real-life problems are much more "intelligent" than their attempts at a worded presentation of the same problems. Clearly the worded problems are complicated by the narration and abstraction of language—a complexity that adds to the challenge.

In one study, 68 percent among a sample of freshmen engineering students translated the following statement incorrectly:

There are six times as many students as professors at this university.

The correct algebraic expression is: $6P = S$

Most of the errors represented the reverse: $6S = P$

Figure 4.10
Graphic Representation of a Word Problem

A dog takes three steps to walk the same distance a cat walks in four steps. Suppose one step of the dog covers $\frac{1}{2}$ foot. How many feet would the cat cover in taking 24 steps?

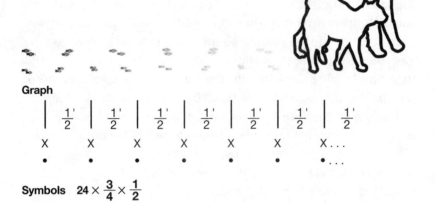

Graph

$$\left| \frac{1'}{2} \right| \frac{1'}{2} \left| \frac{1'}{2} \right| \frac{1'}{2} \left| \frac{1'}{2} \right| \frac{1'}{2} \left| \frac{1'}{2} \right|$$

X   X   X   X   X   X   X . . .

•   •   •   •   •   •   • . . .

Symbols $24 \times \frac{3}{4} \times \frac{1}{2}$

Source: The Math Forum Elementary Problem of the Week, April 19, 1999. Available at http://mathforum.org/elemenpow/solution/solution .ehtml?puzzle=32.

It is possible that in the erroneous case, the letters were used simply as labels. It is also possible that the confusion is associated with the terms of reference that are implied in the language.

The second difficulty of translation is related to the way students associate worded presentations with other representations. The two important factors related to this difficulty are prior experience and the logic of associations (the logic that rules compatibilities and incompatibilities).

Associations are possible only with full understanding of the associates. This means that students will not opt to use a graph if they do not know how to make it, they will not use symbols if symbols make no sense to them, and they will not construct a picture if they cannot produce one that can help them think.

Associations are possible only if the logic that governs them is known. This logic is abstract and has no preference for one representation over the other, yet it holds them together. This logic capitalizes upon relationships, functions, and features. If a student does not understand that a graph or a diagram can present the same relationships between quantities as those presented verbally in the word problem, that a symbol can function in the algebraic expression the same way as in the verbal equivalent, or that a picture features the critical ideas of the worded statement, why should she associate them? Students who have mastered the different representations and the logic of associations among them as external representations can later produce them internally and use them at will to solve word problems. Figure 4.11 illustrates how a drawing can help students visualize multiple solutions.

Figure 4.11
Representation as a Volitional Act

A teacher takes her class of 32 students on a field trip. At lunchtime they stop at a rest area where six large tables and benches are mounted to the cement. Each table can seat six people. How many tables will be full if all the students and their teacher sit around tables to eat their lunches?

There are three possible answers that can be easily considered if one draws the tables and visualizes the possible situation.

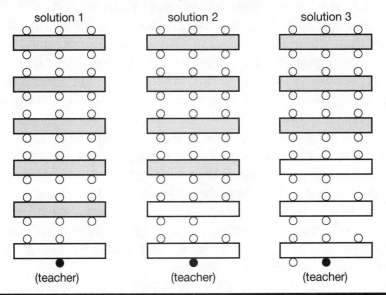

The possibility of choosing among alternative representations may add another complicating factor. It involves setting priorities and making judgments. These processes are subjects of meta-cognitive functions. Such meta-cognitive functions, as they relate to the example above, can be characterized as

1. An awareness of one's own thinking

   I cannot see how the students and the teacher can be seated . . .

2. An awareness of options

   I can draw the table and then see how students can be arranged around the tables . . .

3. An active monitoring of one's cognitive processes

   I will fill up the seats around the tables . . . the last will have only two students and the teacher. Ah, it can have three students and the teacher, and so two tables now are not filled up. Ah, it can have four . . .

4. Ability to regulate one's cognitive processes in relationship to further learning

   Drawing helped me see the solution through . . . It is a good idea to draw something if I can, so I that I may see different solutions.

Where judgment is made about mathematical representations, the consequences must be guarded, as the chosen representation may encounter less restrictive outcomes than in the original presentation. For example, an equation may be less restrictive than the word problem, and some of the solutions may be unreal (complex numbers or negative values that are not possible in the real world). Students who understand this possibility learn to check their conclusions against the original problem.

Teachers must remember that translation among possible problem representations, exercise of judgment about available choices, and recognition of their limitations and restrictions are subjects of learning. These should be matters of discussion and reflection in the classroom, where variations among students provide a valuable resource. They should be matters of divergence and different points of view, in contrast to the typical convergence of mathematical solutions.

Planning the Solution

With increasing complexity, students typically attempt to solve word problems through successive presuppositions, trials, and errors. Such attempts lack determinism and retrospection. They are missing a clear strategy and are never reflected upon after they have been executed. This behavior may be related to a poor definition and formulation of problems (Silver, 1979). Alternatively, it may be related to the failure of meta-cognitive processes to control and monitor appropriate planning (Mevarech & Kramarski, 1997; Schoenfeld, 1994). Before instruction can change such behaviors, it is important for teachers to understand what makes word problems complex and how strategies can address this complexity. In word problems, the number of pieces (components) of information is always smaller than needed to construct complete equations with known numbers. If one piece (component) is missing, then the equation is said to have one unknown and its solution involves one step. In the simple case, problems have no subproblems. However, where two pieces or more of information are unknown, the problem is complex; its solution must involve step-by-step deductions that start from what is known and reveal additional information that is used in subsequent steps until the problem is solved. This process can be described as a solution of consequential subproblems. In algebra, the whole process is formally performed at the outset by the construction of a system of simultaneous equations that involve all the unknowns. In any case, solving complex problems requires developing a sound strategy and executing it carefully throughout the solution process.

A strategy is a general plan of action that, if followed systematically, permits one to solve complex problems. It can often be planned well in advance and must reflect the complexity of a given word problem. It specifies a choice and priority of action for every step of the process. It must define subproblems, the relationships of which may be hierarchical or simultaneous (share a whole or a part), and prioritize them in a way that is logical and economical.

Consider the following example:

Larry owns a rectangular plot of land that is bordered on one side by his neighbor's square plot of land that is 1,000 ft. long, on another side by a ravine that is 2,000 ft. long, on the third side by a row of trees, and on the fourth side by a cliff. Larry wants to divide the plot in half to separate the sheep from the cows, because they have not been getting along. Both the cows and the sheep like to walk down the ravine, but the cows are too timid to try climbing the steep ravine on the way back. Larry has more than enough money to purchase the posts needed to mount a fence between the two halves of his plot. To build a safe and sturdy fence, posts must be placed no more than 4 ft. apart. If the posts cost $8.95 each, how much would it cost him to build the fence?

Strategy:
How does the plot look?
How long is the fence?
How many posts?
Total cost

The strategy guiding the solution to the problem above involves four consequential actions and subproblems. The actions are preconceived and logically prioritized, and they provide the process with intention and a clear sense of closure.

If a complete strategy that is planned in advance is not possible, the alternative is referred to as "trial and error." In this case, trials are used as learning experiences that drive the process "convergingly" toward a solution. This process is common among mathematicians and researchers, and it is often misunderstood to be the same as the random and unsystematic trial-and-error behaviors that characterize low-performing students whose actions do not benefit from their prior experiences.

Planning depends on prior experience with similar types of word problems, but it is always also a matter of managerial decision making that determines the allocation of critical cognitive resources and informs the process. Managerial functions are otherwise referred to as "control processes" (Atkinson & Shiffrin, 1968), "executive functions," or an "executive scheme" (Case, 1974), all covering what we otherwise refer to as meta-cognition. These functions involve the choice of each action and the awareness of its set of preconditions, its set of subactions, and its set of consequences (see Figure 4.12).

Figure 4.12
Meta-Cognition

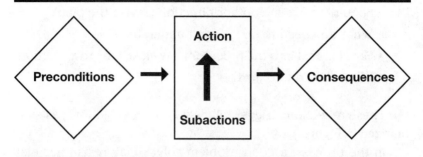

The meta-cognitive system defines such questions about problems and each of their subproblems as follows:

- Is the information sufficient?
- What is relevant?
- What is missing?
- How could the missing information be deduced?

Then it activates the cognitive processes that seek the answers. It executes processes of systematic exploration, comparisons, representation (e.g., drawing), self-monitoring of progress, assessing the validity of interim conclusions, and recognizing when final conclusions are reached.

Solving the Problem

Once a plan has been set for the solution of a word problem, the often extensive and time-consuming hard work of applying it to solving a problem just begins. There are two components to this work: one to do with meta-cognition (purpose) and the other to do with cognition (action). The meta-cognitive component involves online self-checks of the cognitive actions in relation to the plan. This act of self-monitoring is guided by reflections such as the following:

- How am I doing?
- Am I on the right track?
- How should I proceed?

- What should I do to keep track of what I have already done?
- What information is important to remember?
- Should I move in another direction (revise the plan)?
- What do I need to do if I don't understand?
- How far am I into the process? How close am I to a solution?
- What should I do next?

These reflections trigger follow-up cognitive actions, as summarized in Figure 4.13.

In the process, a good problem solver may revise her plan based on how well the plan is working and on what options exist. The ability to do so involves awareness of her own thinking, selective attention, and sustained analysis.

In his research on problem solving, Alan Schoenfeld of the University of California at Berkeley analyzed and compared the way students solved a geometry problem similar to one they had solved just a week earlier to the way a mathematician—who had not worked in geometry for a number of years—solved the same problem. He described the students' attempts as "wild goose

Figure 4.13
Meta-Cognition and Follow-Up Cognitive Functions

Meta-cognitive	Cognitive
• drawing a diagram or model	• representing
• avoiding random trial and error • learning from trial attempts	• generating and testing hypotheses
• looking for patterns	• comparing
• simplifying the problem • using a process of elimination • monitoring	• relating parts to the whole
• working backwards	• testing hypotheses
• estimating	• using logic
• organizing information	• systematic exploring
• writing an equation	• translating, encoding
• recording	• reflective output (nonimpulsive)

chases" lacking meta-cognitive control and guidance, and the mathematician's as "ruthlessly testing and rejecting ideas that were ingeniously generated . . . spending the vast majority of time thinking rather than doing," and "changing directions with new discoveries," eventually successfully solving the problem (Schoenfeld, 1987) (see Figure 4.14).

Such examples show that self-awareness and self-regulation are important determinants of successful problem solving. Without the related meta-cognitive functions, students are easily distracted and cannot exploit what they have learned in the process. These examples imply the important role of teachers in the development of self-awareness and self-regulation by encouraging students to compare, clarify, interpret, and attempt to construct more than one solution. Teachers must guide, coach, and ask insightful questions as well as help students develop independence, rather than limit themselves to evaluating their students' right and wrong answers.

Reviewing the Solution

Often, students terminate the process of solving word problems once they find numerical values that may be substituted for previously unknown values. Many students do not have any idea of what they just found, what "x" stands for, or whether the answer makes sense or not. Some of these students may opt to "solve" the whole problem over again because they are not sure that their numerical conclusion answers the question asked at the outset. Others leave such determinations for the "authorities." This set of behaviors is in part associated with the poor monitoring discussed earlier. It is also representative of uneducated trial and error that precludes possible learning from experience. The alternative behavior is voluntary review of the solution process within the context of the problem.

Looking back at a solution to check the result, check the argument, derive the result differently, use the result or the method for some other problem, reinterpret the problem, interpret the result, or state a new problem is in the focus of what Dewey (1933) and Pólya (1945) described as the most critical step in problem solving. More recently, these behaviors have been the

Figure 4.14
Expert Versus Novice Problem Solving

Episode or Stage Stages, time spent on each stage, sequencing, and management activity by experts

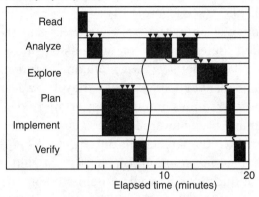

Episode or Stage Stages, time spent on each stage, sequencing, and management activity by novices

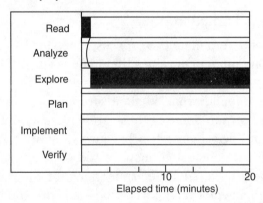

From *Cognitive Science and Mathematics Education* by Alan H. Schoenfeld. © 1987 by Lawrence Erlbaum Associates, Inc., Mahwah, New Jersey. Reprinted with permission.

subject of much research (Schoenfeld, 2002). Today there is ample evidence that solving problems can generate self-learning experiences (Mevarech & Kramarski, 1997; Schoenfeld, 1987). Such learning is important, and it is perhaps the only way to ensure the development of "internal qualities of the mind which structure experiences" as compared to the "out-there-ness" of teacher talk, books, or others' experiences (Thorley, 1990).

Students themselves reviewing their solutions is critical to the construction of their disposition for problem solving.

Reviewing the solution is possible only when one is aware of the problem-solving process. This awareness allows one to review strategies and choices, consolidate methods derived from an episode of mathematics problem solving, and assess the potential for generalizing those methods. Tracing back and correcting errors stimulates the researching and reconstructing of ideas about problem solving and exploiting them in related problems. Researching and reconstructing new ideas about problem solving are guided by reflections such as the following:

- Did my particular course of thinking produce more or less than I had expected?
- What could I have done differently?
- How might I apply this line of thinking to other problems?
- Do I need to go back through the task to fill in any "blanks" in my understanding?
- Can the problem be solved differently?
- Is the solution process different/similar to the solution process of previously solved problems?

Just as the conceptualization of mathematical ideas is not an automatic result of practice, their applications to solving problems are also not automatic. The prevalent view among researchers is that classroom instruction plays an important role in enabling students to solve problems (Vygotsky, 1986). Teachers must encourage students to make generalizations about rules and concepts and engage students in what Feuerstein refers to as mediated learning experiences, which in time become internalized as self-learning and self-activated cognitive and meta-cognitive systems (Feuerstein & Rand, 1997).

Summary

The solving of word problems has come to be the central theme for the mathematics curriculum at all grade levels—as a vision of NCTM standards and state standards for concept-based instruction, and as a matter of concern with the low level of competence and slow progress of U.S. students relative to students in other countries. All experts agree that solving word problems generally presents a significant cognitive challenge that is underestimated by teachers and is not appropriately addressed in instruction.

There is a symbiotic relationship between conceptual development and problem solving. Concepts develop best in the context of problem solving, and solving problems mathematically requires conceptual understanding. Both conceptual development and problem-solving abilities develop together, but developing each requires a different set of didactic considerations. Solving problems mathematically requires the affective dispositions of competence and a host of efficient meta-cognitive and cognitive functions.

Problem solving requires analysis, heuristics, and reasoning that is goal oriented and self-motivated. Students must learn to gather information in careful, systematic, and precise ways. They must understand what they read to be able to define the problem they should pursue. They must break complex problems down to manageable subproblems, set up plans for solving them, and follow their plans rigorously. They must be able to model and represent problems in different ways until the problems make complete sense. They must reflect upon the solutions, compare them, and categorize them with previous experiences. And they must be able to communicate the mathematics and the strategic approaches they use.

Instruction should not seek to automate students' problem solving through the teaching of algorithms and tricks that "work" for given types of problems. Rather it should attempt to provoke students' cognitive dissonance and at the same time enhance cognitive competence. The five components of problem solving that were identified by Pólya in the late 1950s provide a constructive framework for the consideration of the affective, cognitive, and meta-cognitive functions involved. This detailed analysis provides a source of instructional goals and offers structure for what teachers can do to help students become more efficient problem solvers. The next chapter will show how teachers can be best informed on a continual basis about students' failures, successes, and progress.

Chapter 5

Assessment

Formal school assessment traditionally consists of criterion-referenced and norm-referenced tests that are confined to the form of paper-and-pencil, multiple-choice items. Such tests show only whether students can recognize, recall, and apply specific knowledge to solve simple problems. They constitute proxy measures from which the school leadership and policy-makers try to make inferences about the students' knowledge and abilities. The analysis of the test data is focused on the products of learning, not the processes of learning and reasoning. Although they provide some comparative data, criterion-referenced and norm-referenced tests do not provide teachers the feedback they need to revise instruction and improve learning. To the contrary, these tests encourage rudimentary instruction. Experienced teachers who struggle to meet the standards of the formal achievement tests cover what they predict the tests will measure. Because teachers typically teach what tests measure (O'Day & Smith, 1993), professional developers and leaders must promote alternative assessment practices that focus on students' conceptual understanding and problem-solving abilities.

Formal school assessment and typical quizzes and tests are not congruent with the level of conceptual understanding and strategic competencies that are central to Concept-Rich Instruction (Corbett & Wilson, 1991; Shepard & Smith, 1988; Smith & Cohen, 1991). Teachers need to measure students' progress more frequently and less formally than the standards-based academic achievement measures and even the more-frequent, teacher-made quizzes that better reflect instructional objectives. These measures are limited in what they can assess in a short time. They challenge the student to solve simple rather than complex problems, and to reproduce and repeat rather than create original work. All these measures provide teachers only limited assessment of students' ability to solve problems and find new applications for the mathematics they learn. Teachers must use additional assessment tools that inform the processes of learning.

Teachers who follow the practice of Concept-Rich Instruction find alternative assessments that help them identify developmentally appropriate content, recognize student misconceptions, evaluate the meaning students make of what they learn, see whether instruction is effective in altering misconceptions, and distinguish diverse learning needs. These teachers seek assessment tools that help them choose and alternate instructional techniques effectively.

Process Compared to Product-Oriented Assessment

Research shows that where process-oriented alternative assessment is in place, teachers tend to be more flexible and responsive to their students' learning needs (Spinelli, 2001). Furthermore, research shows that teachers who use this type of assessment regularly keep expanding their practices with a greater range of possible choices and strategies (Larrivee, 2000).

Teachers cannot measure directly the processes that underlie reasoning and learning; they can only infer these processes from dialogues with students (Hiebert & Carpenter, 1992). In making such inferences about students' reasoning and learning problems, teachers must align the mathematics knowledge that they target with the situation, types of student responses, and characteristics of the student or group of students. Research shows that teachers who learn to do so tend to create new and better knowledge from their own experiences in teaching than do teachers who rely on traditional assessment (Stein, 2004).

Formative Compared to Summative Assessment

Assessment can provide formative and summative information on student learning. Formative assessment provides feedback on teaching and learning, and summative assessment indicates what students have learned. Summative assessment tools include state and national achievement tests that students take at the end of a year and teacher-made tests given at the end of a unit of study. Formative evaluation involves authentic and dynamic assessment practices. Assessment that is authentic and dynamic mirrors the priorities and challenges of Concept-Rich Instruction, because this form of assessment allows teachers to assess the students' thinking as the students develop their responses to well-designed academic challenges (Wiggins, 1990). Assessment is authentic when teachers directly observe how students analyze, synthesize, and apply what they have learned in a substantial manner to solving complex problems. It is dynamic when it shows not only what the student knows, but also how the student learns.

Formative assessment may include interviews with individuals and small groups of students, student journals, student self-assessment, portfolios, performance assessment, and surveys. Because the various methods of assessment provide different types of information, teachers must learn to employ and integrate the information they gather from them.

Formative assessment may take different forms, but it usually includes a task and a rubric by which performance is evaluated. The task involves meaningful problems from real-world contexts. The rubric is always based on the teacher's understanding of the specific characteristics that make up good performance and identifies milestones of learning. The rubric also guides students to better develop the skills and understanding that are necessary to perform well.

Classroom Communication and Observations

Classroom communication and observations vary in form and purpose. Teachers can observe students as they discuss and debate mathematical ideas and solutions to problems, they can watch students as they model and explain their solutions on the board, and they can interact with individual students while they are engaged in classroom assignments. For example, observations are particularly well suited for assessing students' concept and skills of measurement. Teachers can observe students measure length, width, height, weight, capacity, volume, area, time, and temperature using standard units. They can examine whether students understand the importance of a point of reference for measurement. They can engage students in comparisons by asking which ball is heavier, which stick is longer, which of two different-shaped containers holds more water, whether a wrapping paper of a certain area can completely cover a given box, and so forth.

When the level of students' receptive and expressive language is appropriate, classroom discussions may reveal important information about students' understanding and ability to apply their mathematics knowledge. The revelation is even more acute when students see themselves not just as responders to questions, but also as posers of questions. In the case of students with limited English proficiency, teachers must rely more heavily on assessment tools that are focused on activities rather than classroom dialogue. Teachers who learn to listen to the informal language that students use in the classroom while they develop concepts and skills can identify mathematical preconcepts and misconceptions that always crop up in these contexts.

If teachers create a classroom culture in which the most struggling students feel comfortable exposing their thinking in front of their peers, teachers can then engage their students in problem solving, watch them model solutions on the board, ask questions, and listen to the students' answers. In this environment teachers can effectively probe the reasons behind students' actions, behaviors, and language. In the absence of this desirable environment, teachers must resort to assessment in the context of individual problem-based activities.

Teachers can also assess learning while individual students are engaged in classroom assignments. Here, teachers must assume the role of a participant-observer—they are part of and live in the learning community, but maintain a neutral posture. They may encourage students and praise their work; however, if they want to assess learning, they should not ask leading questions. To assess learning teachers must ask only open-ended questions and maintain a neutral posture regarding students' answers. Teachers must always avoid disturbing students when they are working intently.

Classroom observations can help teachers assess their students' understanding and ability to apply mathematical concepts, their ability to solve problems, their ability to communicate mathematically, and their ability to work with others. Any classroom observation is valuable if it is articulated by, and is limited to, specific goals and is void of extraneous information—to the extent that teachers collect and manage their assessment for future reference.

Teachers can use several effective and efficient means for collecting observation information. They can use note cards or a small, pocket-sized tape recorder for dictating observations; use

Figure 5.1

Teacher's Checklist for Cognitive Behaviors
of Word Problem Solving in Geometry

Input	Comments
Collects and organizes data systematically	Integer, fraction, percent, decimal, ratio, exponent, inverse, rate, distance, perimeter, area, surface-area, volume, angle, radius, rectangular-solid, cylinder, pyramid, cone, sphere, prime-factor (multiple), symmetry, congruency, similarity, perpendicularity, parallelism, reflection, flip, slide, turn, enlargement, mean, median, mode
Understands vocabulary	
	Tables, graphs, symbols
Understands nonverbal expressions	
Names geometric figures (including solids)	

continued

Figure 5.1, continued

Input	Comments
Is reflective (not impulsive) when performing a complex task	
Is precise	Measures, estimates
Analyzes the properties of and relationships within two- and three-dimensional geometric figures	

Elaboration	Comments
Identifies and defines problems	
Projects relationships	
Compares	Part-whole, relative terms, concrete and symbolic representations, units of measurement
Coordinates several variables simultaneously	Problem solving, coordinate geometry, comparison of geometric shapes by several variables
Finds causal relationships	
Plans ahead	
Forms hypotheses and tests them logically	
Uses logic to reach valid conclusions	Inference, induction (generalization), deductive

Output	Comments
Considers communication from the receiver's point of view	Clear responses
Uses vocabulary properly to communicate mathematics ideas	Integer, fraction, percent, decimal, ratio, exponent, inverse, rate, distance, perimeter, area, surface-area, volume, angle, radius, rectangular-solid, cylinder, pyramid, cone, sphere, prime-factor (multiple), symmetry, congruency, similarity, perpendicularity, parallelism, reflection, flip, slide, turn, enlargement, mean, median, mode
Uses nonverbal expressions to communicate	Tables, graphs, symbols
Presents data in an orderly way	
Communicates complete ideas	

a video camera; and develop and use checklists of desired concepts and actions. Figure 5.1 presents an example of a checklist that a mathematics teacher prepared based on her knowledge of Feuerstein's classification of cognitive functions (Feuerstein, Rand, Hoffman, & Miller, 1994).

Teachers do not have to observe each student every day. Rather, to the extent possible, teachers should designate a time for each student to be observed and focus on that particular student during that time. Furthermore, because teachers use additional assessment methods, they may want to limit their classroom observations to the assessment of progress in particular areas of mathematics with particular students.

In conjunction with other forms of classroom communication, such as small-group and whole-class discussions, teachers can use surveys to collect academic, as well as affective, information. In particular, teachers can use surveys periodically to assess changes in students' affective mathematical dispositions, attitudes, efficacy, and anxieties. Such surveys may consist of Likert scale ratings and open-ended items.

Classroom communication and observations are integral to Concept-Rich Instruction, and when appropriate, teachers should share their observations with students to alter students' misconceptions. When teachers do so, new learning begins. Hence, by its nature, classroom observation is a method of dynamic assessment.

Analyzing Student Homework

Homework is assigned independent practice. It is generally designed to reinforce classroom learning, teach students to independently apply newly acquired skills and knowledge, and develop their study skills and personal responsibility. Homework may help students to review and practice what they have learned, prepare them for the next day's class, and engage them in investigating topics more fully than classtime allows. Research shows that where homework is routinely assigned and evaluated, students tend to have higher achievement (LaConte,

1981; Lindsay, Greathouse, & Nye, 1988; Walberg, Paschal, & Weinstein, 1985).

Research on effective homework practice shows that teachers should

- Teach students how to organize their work.
- Vary homework assignments.
- Ensure that students understand the assignment and are sufficiently prepared for the homework assignment.
- Make sure students understand the learning value of the assignment.
- Assign homework that is not overly long.
- Give recognition to students for completion of homework assignments.
- Check homework for understanding and modify instruction accordingly.
- Be clear on how homework assignments will be evaluated.
- Have students exchange and correct homework assignments in class.
- Provide feedback quickly and routinely on individual students' progress.
- Involve parents.

(England & Flatley 1985; Good & Grouws, 1979)

Besides additional learning experiences, homework assignments provide teachers with important data that they can use to diagnose students' learning problems. In fact, school reformers at Harvard Project Zero, the Annenberg Institute for School Reform, and the Coalition for Better Schools argue that analyzing student work is key to improving teaching and accountability. They argue for refocusing professional development on reflective examination of authentic student work, rather than on test scores and grades, as representations of student learning (Allen, 1998; Blythe, Allen, & Powell, 1999).

To best assess their students' work, teachers may require that students record not only their solutions to home and classroom assignments, but also maintain a problem-solving notebook with weekly entries, including the following:

- A discussion of the strategies they used to solve the problem.
- A comparison of the mathematical similarities among problems.
- Possible extensions for the problem.
- An investigation of at least one of the possible extensions.
- Reflection about their feelings about a solution.

Teachers can assess students' abilities and difficulties by analyzing students' work samples and from the students' reflections as self-reported. In the case of students who cannot complete their homework or students who complete their work incorrectly, teachers must look closely at the homework and may have to compare it to other samples of the students' work to find the reasons and adjust instruction accordingly.

Individual Interviews
Around Problem-Solving Activities

What researchers know today about student errors comes from studies that focus on the ways individual students process information. Researchers often study errors through clinical interviews. This method of research is important because it helps identify general issues of learning and learning problems as well as what constitutes effective instruction. However, it is also important because it provides a model for an alternative assessment strategy that teachers can use in their classrooms. The particular significance of interviews is that they can reveal to teachers the differences between their and their students' values, concepts, guiding theories, and problem-solving strategies in doing math. If teachers consistently apply what is learned from student interviews in the classroom, they will improve their instructional practices.

Researchers use the clinical interview as a three-stage methodology for constructing and testing hypotheses regarding individuals' alternative conceptions. In the first stage, the interviewer formulates hypotheses of a particular reasoning and tests these hypotheses through probes. In the second stage, several researchers independently analyze the recorded interviews and arrive at agreed-upon hypotheses. These hypotheses are then subjected to further testing in the third stage. It is a rigorous process that must meet the scientific standards of validity and reliability, and researchers do not apply it lightly. However, teachers could use clinical interviews as an alternative assessment tool if they know their students, know the typical misconceptions, use the method repeatedly with some students, and follow a set of guidelines such as the one listed below.

Teachers can design interviews that help identify the learning needs of individual students. The interviews allow teachers to follow their students as the students model mathematical concepts and skills and communicate them mathematically; to learn about student misconceptions and guide students toward more complex ideas; to investigate whether students have appropriately generalized a concept; and to find out whether students can apply concepts to new problems. For example, a teacher can use an interview to assess the understanding of place value. He may ask a student to model number names with place value blocks and a place value mat. The student may name 502 as 500 and two ones; 50 tens and two ones; or five hundreds, zero tens, and two ones. Or, the teacher may find out that the student does not understand the role of zero as a placeholder. In this case, the teacher can use probing questions to guide the student toward further learning and help the student attend to misunderstandings. The teacher may also ask the student to model and explain the process for adding 57 and 34. At the end of the interview, the teacher may engage the student in solving a real-world, nonroutine word problem and watch as the student applies the concepts of place value through modeling and explaining the process she performs.

Because a heavy classload may prohibit them from using this tool with all students, teachers may conduct individual interviews with a selective few of their students to sample their class's progress with problem solving (Long & Ben-Hur, 1991). Teachers may want to assess the learning problems of students who previously tested poorly or students who perform poorly in class, and perhaps compare their performance with the performance of students who are highly proficient. When appropriate—and to save time—teachers could use the procedure with small groups of students. In this case, teachers ought to prepare specific assessment goals for the individuals as well as for the group.

Interviews may target a variety of goals:

- Identifying student misconceptions in a particular area of mathematics.
- Determining the depth and breadth of a student's proficiency as a mathematical problem solver. For example—
  — Do students define the problem they are about to solve?
  — How do they evaluate the type and difficulty level of the problem?
  — How do they select an algorithm?
  — How effective are the meta-cognitive processes?
  — Are the students confident about their solutions?
  — Is there divergent thinking?
  — Do students have a self-concept as being able to solve mathematics problems?
  — How do students learn best?

Interviews may also provide opportunities to assess students' ability to communicate using mathematics as a language. At the same time, teachers should know that students frequently know more mathematics than they can communicate verbally (Siegler, 2003), and therefore teachers should always probe when they want to properly evaluate students' mathematical knowledge.

In addition, individual and small-group interviews provide opportunities for students to ask questions that they may not otherwise ask in a large-group setting.

For interviews to be effective, teachers must prepare ahead of time. They must choose and analyze problems in terms of the National Council of Teachers of Mathematics (NCTM) standards they may want to use, mathematics concepts and operations, and the cognitive behaviors that the problems challenge.

The effective interview begins with a set-up that relieves the student's anxiety:

- Use a quiet and comfortable space.
- Calm the student by telling her that the evaluator (teacher) will help her succeed.
- Indicate that the purpose is NOT to evaluate the student, but to evaluate the effectiveness of instruction.
- Answer all questions the student may have before the interview.
- Explain the interview process.
- Ask the student to help set up the interview.
- Praise cooperation.

Once the interview starts, teachers must be flexible. They must be ready to alter tasks and offer just enough help. The student should always complete at least some of the tasks and be pleased with her accomplishment. Teachers must ask questions that do not lead. Rather, they should

- Ask open-ended questions.
- Wait patiently for responses.
- Remain nonjudgmental to gain further insight into the student's thought process.
- Ask the student to clarify or explain surprising answers.
- Follow up with questions until student thinking is clear.

Teachers must also maintain uninterrupted dialogue, and avoid, if possible, phone calls, announcements over loud speakers, bell sounds, and so forth. Teachers should

- Reveal their interest and excitement about the student's work.
- Refrain from taking notes in the course of the interview (videotaping can help).
- Listen carefully.

Finally, teachers should conclude the interview on a high note, such as

- Telling the student how and explain why they enjoyed the interview.
- Inviting the student to come to them if she needs help.
- Promising to interview her again from time to time.

Journal Writing

Journal writing encourages students to monitor, review, and reflect upon their learning experiences. Thus, it helps students develop concepts, skills, and strategies for solving a variety of new problems. As a result of the reflective process that is involved in writing journals, students learn to view mathematics as more than just an exercise in getting the right answer. At the same time, journals can help teachers assess students' reflections of their own capabilities, attitudes, and dispositions and evaluate their abilities to communicate mathematically through writing.

To benefit the most from student journals, a teacher must develop together with the students a purpose for journal entries. For example, journals entries could include

- Problems that students want to solve
- Solution processes
- Presentation of alternative solution processes (if appropriate)
- Presentation of alternative solutions to the problem (if appropriate)
- Reflection on problem-solving strategies
- Discussion of the validity of the solution
- Definition of mathematical concepts and describing their meaning
- Identification of skills that students have developed from experience
- Reflections on the problem-solving experience

- Checklists to record such things as new learning tools and new problem-solving strategies
- Feelings students have about being able to solve the problem

Students should be encouraged to use in their journals language such as the following:

"This was possible because . . . Alternatively . . ."

"The problem here, I believe, was that . . ."

"While it may be true that . . ."

"On the one hand . . ."

"In thinking back . . ."

"On reflection . . ."

"I guess that this problem has made me aware of . . ."

Because the focus of journal entries may differ from time to time, teachers should always encourage students to keep their records in an orderly notebook and review, relate, and compare current journal entries to previous ones.

Journals are most valuable as learning tools if students discuss their records and teachers have opportunities to reinforce or intervene in the process by probing, suggesting new directions for reflection, challenging misconceptions, or questioning the efficiency strategies. Journals are also most valuable if students share them with each other. At the same time that journals facilitate learning, journal entries provide insight into how students are developing as problem solvers and how teachers might enhance their development.

Although journal writing provides opportunities for student reflection, there are difficulties associated with using journal writing as evidence of learning. Journal entries are not easy to analyze for assessment purposes. There is always the possibility that the reader's perceptions and expectations may alter the authentic meaning of the personal, reactive, emotive, and, at the time of writing, not-at-all reflective student statements. However, there is no doubt that student journals could be one source of information among others.

Student Self-Assessment

There is general agreement that students' ability to monitor and assess their own learning is important, and that this ability must be cultivated in the classroom. Students do not learn to monitor and assess their own work in classrooms that place a premium on obtaining the correct answers. Students do so only if they are unafraid to risk exposing their errors and misconceptions, and if the outcomes of self-assessment are rewarding. Self-monitoring and self-assessment develop when teachers show students exactly what is meant by assessment and emphasize that assessment does not necessarily imply grading. Self-monitoring and self-assessment develop when teachers help students identify the criteria that guide their monitoring and assessment (e.g., a rubric).

For example, Ms. G. assigned a project to group 5 to calculate how many pennies would have to be stacked on top of each other from the ground up until the pile reached the middle of the St. Louis Gateway Arch. Then students had to calculate the amount of money these coins were worth in dollars and estimate the volume of a container that could carry the coins from the bank to the site. She gave the group the necessary dimensions of the arch and assigned an individual responsibility for each group member. Individual responsibilities might include leader, facilitator, recorder, reporter, and timekeeper. Because the solution the group arrived at did not meet the required conditions, the teacher encouraged the students to alter their plans and try again. After completing the task, the students had to record which concepts and which strategies they used to solve the problem. Each student had to assess whether or not the solution met the required conditions. Eventually the students had to evaluate how they worked as a team.

In addition to its important function as a tool of learning, self-assessment that students share with teachers may also offer teachers a source of valuable assessment data. Because self-assessment that is guided by specific criteria is still subjective, it provides experienced teachers access to their students' awareness of their misconceptions and weak strategic competencies and to their self-concept as mathematics learners. In fact, student self-monitoring and self-assessment may provide teachers with assessment information that may not be available through any other assessment tool.

Portfolio Assessment

Portfolio assessment is a method by which students demonstrate their ability to do major pieces of work that are more elaborate and time-consuming than short exercises. The Assessment Standards for School Mathematics recognizes this form of assessment as a good example of integration of instruction and assessment activities. As a process-oriented approach to assessment, portfolios can link successes and failures to performance and facilitate goal setting and self-motivated learning. Although more subjective than traditional testing, portfolios indicate student choices and interpretations and may reveal how students think and why.

Teachers can make valid inferences about the progress in students' understanding of concepts and skills from examinations of dated work samples in students' portfolios. For example, a portfolio that contains a student's work samples in plane geometry might include the following:

- Constructions of paper or geoboard models that represent plane figures.
- Written definitions and descriptions of plane figures.
- Identification of plane figures in the environment.
- Classifications of plane figures.
- Records of investigations, explorations, and discussions of geometry concepts.

The portfolio may show initial sketches and records of improper identification of designated plane figures. Later records in this portfolio may indicate the student's better understanding of the geometry concepts, and the latest records may show complete understanding.

Teachers may guide their students' work on developing their portfolios through the following strategies:

- Asking open-ended questions.
- Assigning reports of group projects.
- Initiating work from another subject area that involves mathematics problem solving.
- Posing problems.
- Encouraging students to include excerpts of reflections on mathematics problem solving from their daily journal.
- Challenging students to draft, revise, and prepare final versions of their work on a complex mathematics problem.
- Asking students to assemble and include in their portfolio newspaper and magazine articles featuring mathematics problems.
- Encouraging students to include papers that show their corrections of errors or misconceptions.
- Providing checklists.

There are three types of mathematics assessment portfolios: the showcase portfolio, the teacher-student portfolio, and the teacher alternative assessment portfolio (Columba & Dolgos, 1995).

- A showcase portfolio focuses on the student's best and most representative work. The important characteristic of this portfolio is that it features what students themselves select as representative of their work.
- A teacher-student portfolio, otherwise referred to as a "working portfolio" or a a "working folder," is a product of collaboration between the teacher and student. Its value as an assessment tool is in the maintenance of a record of communication with the student.
- A teacher alternative assessment portfolio is used solely as an assessment tool. This focused portfolio contains scored, rated, ranked, or evaluated work and provides a holistic assessment.

When teachers give students the opportunity to choose the portfolio contents, the students' choices give teachers insights into students' interpretation of their work, their dispositions toward mathematics, and their mathematical understanding. Furthermore, because the portfolio contents are developed over time, teachers can learn not only the current state of students' learning, but also the individual student's learning patterns.

Portfolio assessments may provide teachers and students with valuable insights into students' learning progress if they contain accurate and detailed accounts of the students' work and if they are maintained over time. Both these conditions are hard to meet, as portfolio assessment consumes more time than other forms of assessment.

Performance-Based Assessment

Performance-based assessment involves individual or group projects around a mathematical problem. The problem may take from a half hour to several days to solve, and the students' activities are often videotaped or audiotaped. The goal is to assess both the process and product of the student's or group's solution of the problem.

The teacher guides the assessment along the following steps:

- Presents students with a problem related to what they are already doing in class.
- Observes what students are doing and saying and takes anecdotal notes about students' actions that exemplify the criteria set.
- Interviews students during or after the activity.
- Asks students to write about the problem or in response to a specific question on the problem, and then collects the students' writings.
- Scores the students' work against a set of performance criteria.

As part of, or in addition to, the above, the teacher may ask students to discuss strategies they used to solve the problem, compare problems, propose possible extensions for the problem, and reflect upon their feeling about their experience with the problem. Over time, performance-based assessment should also reveal whether students value mathematics, are confident in their ability to use mathematics to solve problems, and are learning to communicate mathematically.

Performance-based assessment provides teachers information on their students' thinking and understanding, like the other forms of alternative assessments that have been discussed. It should also help students gain insight into their own learning and understanding of mathematics. It is important that teachers encourage students to monitor their learning and evaluate their strategies and their current levels of understanding. Feedback should occur continuously, but not intrusively, as part of instruction. Teachers should carefully consider if formal or informal feedback will be most constructive.

Summary

Summative assessment is limited to the products of students' learning. It is time-consuming and yields little benefit to students' learning. Only by inference does such assessment provide information on students' conceptual understanding and reasoning. Therefore, Concept-Rich Mathematics Instruction promotes using a variety of formative assessment methods that can better reveal the state of students' learning. Because formative assessment is contextualized in learning, it does not consume instructional time without yielding direct benefits to students. It is authentic and dynamic, and therefore it is constructive to classroom learning and teaching.

Formative assessment not only targets the acquisition of new concepts and skills, it also identifies students' interests in mathematics, the meaning that students find in concepts, students' preconceptions and misconceptions, levels of strategic competency, and students' ability to communicate mathematically. It also reveals changes in the students' affective dispositions, their attitudes and anxieties, and their sense of responsibility for learning. Formative assessment also provides opportunities for teachers to test the effects of new instructional strategies.

However, formative assessment is not simple to perform with any regularity. To conduct formative assessment, teachers must learn how to systematically and continually collect and organize data while managing time and resources. They must learn how to generate opportunities for assessment and use a variety of tools. They must learn to act as participant-observers with small groups of students, ask open-ended questions, listen, and remain nonjudgmental as students reflect on their actions. Teachers must learn how to use interviews with individual students to assess learning difficulties; how to challenge students to self-monitor and self-assess their learning, while encouraging them to share their assessment; how to objectively analyze homework assignments and portfolios; and how to conduct performance-based assessment to find meaningful signs of progress in students' learning.

Teachers can conduct formative assessment in the course of classroom activities; in private meetings with individual students, parents, or other teachers; and while analyzing student artifacts after school. But they must learn to organize the various formative assessment data and integrate these data with information generated from different summative assessment tools. The combination of formative and summative assessment data will help teachers to better understand how students progress and what they need to learn more effectively to meet new learning goals.

Students benefit from formative assessment as well. Most of the tools and methods of formative assessment involve students' reflections and heightened awareness. In the process of active engagement in the assessment of their knowledge and skills, students may find new meanings; recognize their misconceptions; and find out that there are different representations, strategies, or points of view than they originally considered. They may learn how to learn and may become more involved in, and take more responsibility for, their own learning.

Afterword

Concept-Rich Instruction is based on the prevalent constructivist view that concepts are not simply facts to be memorized and later recalled, but knowledge that is featured in cognitive structures. Concept-Rich Instruction emphasizes the critical role of mediation in conceptual development and underscores the importance of the verbal and reflective features of classroom interaction.

In Concept-Rich Instruction, teachers must first identify the core concepts of the mathematics curriculum and plan an instructional sequence that builds upon concepts students already understand and gradually engages students in further learning. Teachers design learning experiences that provoke thoughtful discussions that lead to new mathematical concepts and prepare students to apply these concepts on their own.

From the view of Concept-Rich Instruction, learning mathematics reflects a progression from preconceptions to more encompassing and more appropriate concepts. Therefore, teachers must consider student errors, particularly systematic errors that are generated by preconceptions, as important sources of information and as key instructional tools. To correct student misconceptions, teachers should conduct classroom dialogues that are reciprocal, flexible, rich with alternative representations, provocative and reflective, verbally clear, and constructive. Concept-Rich Instruction works best in the context of problem-solving activities. In this context, teachers provoke students' cognitive dissonance and at the same time mediate their cognitive competence.

The assessments used in Concept-Rich Instruction include a variety of formative methods that can reveal the state of students' learning. The targets of assessments include students' interest, the meaning they find in what they learn, their preconceptions, their strategic competency; their ability to communicate mathematically, their attitudes and anxieties, and their motivation. Formative assessment provides opportunities for teachers to test the effects of new instructional strategies and opportunities for students to reflect upon their learning.

Schools and teachers who adopt Concept-Rich Instruction will effect the greatest improvement of students' mathematical performance and move closer to fulfillment of the NCTM standards. Such a move will not come easily. It will require not only a shift in teachers' methodology, but also, for many, a substantive change in understanding, belief, and attitude about the role of thinking and problem solving in learning mathematics, as well as in the capabilities of all students (including those who are currently not performing well) to think mathematically and solve challenging problems and in their willingness to do so. To bring about these changes in teachers, school districts will need to make equally substantive changes in the quantity and quality of professional development that they provide to teachers of mathematics, and to their coaches and mentors and their supervisors. Likewise, colleges and universities will need to change their approach to mathematics education. The NCTM standards provide the foundation for these changes. I hope that this book provides the first building blocks for constructing a new edifice, the edifice of Concept-Rich Instruction, that will return mathematics achievement in the United States to first-class status in the education of its children.

Description of Teacher Activity

DESCRIPTION OF TEACHER ACTIVITY	NO OPPORTUNITY	MISSED OPPORTUNITY	USUALLY IMPLEMENTED	SOMETIMES IMPLEMENTED	NEGATION	
Practice						
1. Teacher explains value of practice.						
2. Students express need for additional practice.						
3. Practice is done with variable tasks.						
4. Practice is sufficient. (Students master the use of a new concept.)						
5. Students master the application of a concept in variable tasks.						
6. Conceptual errors (misconceptions) are eliminated from the students' work.						
Decontextualization						
1. Teacher encourages reflective discussions that elicit possible misconceptions.						
2. Students apply the new concept voluntarily to variable tasks.						
3. Teacher creates a nonthreatening environment for the analysis of students' errors.						
4. Teacher encourages students to analyze errors in terms of the new concept.						
5. Students stop to look for hints, specific key words, and teacher's support for the application of the new concept.						
Meaning						
1. Teacher encourages students to use the terms *always* and *never* as they discuss their learning.						
2. Teacher encourages students to find the consistency in the application of a new concept in various instances.						
3. Teacher encourages students to verbally explain, not just show, their work.						
4. Teacher encourages students to discuss new concepts, not just appy the concept.						
5. Teacher uses students' reflective discussions to evaluate the development of the meaning of new concepts.						

DESCRIPTION OF TEACHER ACTIVITY	NO OPPORTUNITY	MISSED OPPORTUNITY	USUALLY IMPLEMENTED	SOMETIMES IMPLEMENTED	NEGATION	
Recontextualization						
1. Teacher waits for student responses to concept-forming questions long enough to encourage all students to form answers.						
2. Teacher encourages students to develop their own applications for new concepts.						
3. Teacher encourages the development of variable applications.						
4. Teacher responds neutrally to a student's idea, but encourages its critical analysis by peers in accordance with the new concept.						
5. Teacher encourages students to evaluate their understanding of new concepts.						
Realization						
1. Teacher encourages the development of variable applications in students' daily life.						
2. Teacher encourages students to participate in (and later report on) the use of the newly learned concept.						
3. Teacher encourages students to suggest uses of a new concept across the curriculum.						
4. Teacher shares with other teachers the mastery of the new concept and encourages other teachers to use it in their lessons.						
5. Teacher shares with parents the students' mastery of new concepts and encourages them to engage their children in using them in daily life.						

Major Mathematical Concepts for Grades 6–8

Major Mathematical Concepts for Grades 6–8

I = Introduce Concept   M = Maintain Concept

	Grade 6	Grade 7	Grade 8
Algebra and Algebraic Thinking	Properties		Properties of Rational Numbers (I)
	Expressions		
	Equations		
	Functions (I)	Absolute Value (I)	Step (I)
	Graphing: Integers and Functions (I)	Inequalities and Slope (I)	Inequalities (I)
	Integers	Absolute Value, Multiply and Divide, Equations (I)	
			Polynomials
			Rational, Irrational, and Real Numbers (I)
	Decimals (M)		
	Scientific Notation (I)		
	Fractions (M)		
Geometry and Spatial Reasoning	Angles (M)		
	Constructions: Congruent Segment, Parallel and Perpendicular Lines (I)	Perpendicular and Angle Bisectors, Congruent Angles (I)	
	Polygons: Different View (I)	Pythagoren Theorem (I)	
	Transformations: Translations, Rotations, Reflections (I)		Dilations (I)
	Coordinate Geometry (I)		

continued

Major Mathematical Concepts for Grades 6–8 (continued)

I = Introduce Concept   M = Maintain Concept

	Grade 6	Grade 7	Grade 8
Measurement	Area: Composite Figures (I)	Composite Figures and Trapezoids (I)	
	Surface Area: Prisms (I)	Cylinders (I)	
	Volume	Volume: Cylinders (I)	Volume: Cones, Pyramids, Spheres (I)
	Indirect Measurement: Scale Drawing, Using Similar Triangles, Ratio in Right Triangles (I)	Pythagorean Theorem (I)	Trigonometric Ratios (I)
Number Sense and Quantitative Reasoning	Compare and Order: Integers (I)		Rationals and Irrationals (I)
	Exponents	Negative Numbers (I)	
	Scientific Notation		
		Square Number and Square Roots (I)	
Probability	Independent and Dependent Events	Odds (I)	
	Theoretical Probability (I)		
	Probability of Complements		
	Permutation and Combinations		Factorial Notation and Pascal's Triangle (I)
Proportional Reasoning	Ratios	Equal Ratios (I)	
	Rate: Unit Price (I)		Dimensional Analysis (I)
	Proportions		
	Proportions in Similar Figures		
	Percentages		

References

Allen, D. (Ed.). (1998). *Assessing student learning: From grading to understanding*. New York: Teachers College Press.

Anderson, J. R. (1995). *Cognitive psychology and its implications* (4th ed.). New York: W. H. Freeman and Company.

Asiala, M., Brown, A., DeVries, D., Dubinsky, E., Mathews, D., & Thomas, K. (1996). A framework for research and curriculum development in undergraduate mathematics education (pp. 1–32), CBMS Issues in Mathematics Education (Vol. 6). In A.H. Schoenfeld, J. Kaput, & E. Dubinsky (Eds.), *Research in College Mathematics Education*. Providence, RI: American Mathematical Society.

Atkinson, R., & Shiffrin, M. (1968). Human memory: A proposed system and its control processes. In G. H. Bower & J. T. Spence (Eds.), *The psychology of learning and motivation: Advances in theory and research* (Vol. 2). New York: Academic Press.

Baird, J. R., Fensham, P. J., Gunstone, R. F., & White, R. T. (1991). The importance of reflection in improving science teaching and learning. *Journal of Research in Science Teaching, 28*(2), 163–182.

Ball, D. L., & Bass, H. (2000). Making believe: The construction of public mathematical knowledge in the elementary classroom. In D. Phillips (Ed.), *Constructivism in education* (pp. 193–224). Chicago: University of Chicago Press.

Bartsch, R. (1998). *Dynamic conceptual semantics: A logico-philosophical investigation into concept formation and understanding*. Stanford, CA: CSLI Publications.

Baxter, J. (1989). Children's understanding of familiar astronomical events. *International Journal of Science Education, 11*(5), 502–512.

Beeth, M. E. (1993, April). *Classroom environment and conceptual change instruction*. Paper presented at the annual meeting of the National Association of Research in Science Teaching, Atlanta, GA.

Bell, A. W., Fischbein, E., & Greer, B. (1984). Choice of operation in verbal arithmetic problem: The effects of number size, problem structure and content. *Educational Studies in Mathematics, 15*(2), 129–147.

Ben-Hur, M. (Ed.) (1994) *On Feuerstein's Instrumental Enrichment: A collection*. Arlington Heights, IL.:IRI/SkyLight Training and Publishing, Inc.

Ben-Hur, M. (2004). *Forming early concepts of mathematics: A manual for successful mathematics teaching*. Glencoe, IL: International Renewal Institute, Inc.

Ben-Hur, M. (2004). *Investigating the big ideas of arithmetic: A manual for successful mathematics teaching*. Glencoe, IL: International Renewal Institute, Inc.

Ben-Hur, M. (2004). *Overcoming the challenge of geometry: A manual for successful mathematics teaching*. Glencoe, IL: International Renewal Institute, Inc.

Ben-Hur, M. (2004). *Making algebra accessible to all: A manual for successful mathematics teaching*. Glencoe, IL: International Renewal Institute, Inc.

Ben-Hur, M. (2004). *Mediating probability and statistics: A manual for successful mathematics teaching*. Glencoe, IL: International Renewal Institute, Inc.

Biggs, J., & Collins, K. (1982). *Evaluating the quality of learning: The SOLO taxonomy*. New York: Academic Press.

Blythe, T., Allen, D., & Powell, B. S. (1999). *Looking together at student work: A companion guide to assessing student learning*. New York: Teachers College Press.

Borovcnik, M., & Bentz, H. J. (1991). Empirical research in understanding probability. In R. Kapadia & M. Borovcnik (Eds.), *Chance encounters: Probability in education* (pp. 73–105). Dordrecht, The Netherlands: Kluwer Academic Publishers.

Bransford, J. D., Brown, A. L., & Cocking, R. R. (Eds.). (1999). *How people learn: Brain, mind, experience, and school.* Washington, DC: National Academy Press.

Brown, J. S., & Burton, R. R. (1978). Diagnostic models for procedural bugs in basic mathematical skills. *Cognitive Science, 2*(1), 155–192.

Bruner, J. (1991). *Acts of meaning.* Cambridge, MA: Harvard University Press.

Bunge, M. (1962). *Intuition and science.* New York: Prentice-Hall.

Byrnes, J., & Wasik, B. (1991). Role of conceptual knowledge in mathematical procedural learning. *Developmental Psychology, 27*(5), 777–786.

Campbell, K. J., Collis, K. F., & Watson, J. M. (1993). Multimodal functioning during mathematical problem solving. In B. Atweh, C. Kanes, M. Carss, & G. Booker (Eds.), *Contexts in mathematics education* (pp. 147–151). Brisbane, Australia: Mathematics Education Research Group of Australasia.

Campbell, K. J., Collis, K. F., & Watson, J. M. (1995). Visual processing during mathematical problem solving. *Educational Studies in Mathematics, 28*(2), 177–194.

Carpenter, T. P. (1989). Teaching as problem solving. In R. I. Charles & E. A. Silver (Eds.), *The teaching and assessing of mathematical problem solving* (pp.187–202). Reston, VA: National Council of Teachers of Mathematics.

Carpenter, T. P., Ansel, E., Franke, M. L., Fennema, E., & Wiesbeck, L. (1993). Models of problem solving: A study of kindergarten children's problem-solving processes. *Journal for Research in Mathematics Education, 24*(5), 428–441.

Carpenter, T. P., Fennema, E., Franke, M. L., Empson, S. B., & Levy, L. W. (1999). *Children's mathematics: Cognitively guided instruction.* Portsmouth, NH: Heinemann.

Carpenter, T. P., Fennema, E., Peterson, P. L., Chiang, C. P., & Loef, M. (1989). Using knowledge of children's mathematics thinking in classroom teaching: An experimental study. *American Educational Research Journal, 26*(4), 499–531.

Carpenter, T. P., & Lehrer, R. (1999). Teaching and learning mathematics with understanding. In E. Fennema & T. A. Romberg (Eds.), *Mathematics classrooms that promote understanding* (pp. 19–32). Mahwah, NJ: Lawrence Erlbaum Associates.

Case, R. (1974). Structures and strictures: Some functional limitations on the course of cognitive growth. *Cognitive Psychology, 6*(4), 544–574.

Cawley, J. F., Fitzmaurice-Hayes, A. M., & Shaw, R. A. (1988). *Mathematics for the mildly handicapped: A guide to curriculum and instruction* (p. 174). Boston: Allyn and Bacon.

Clement, J. (1993). Using bridging analogies and anchoring intuitions to deal with students' preconceptions in physics. *Journal of Research in Science Teaching, 30*(10), 1241–1257.

Columba, L., & Dolgos, K. A. (1995). Portfolio assessment in mathematics. *Reading Improvement, 32*(3), 174–176.

Cook, M. (2001). Mathematics: The thinking arena for problem-solving. In A. Costa (Ed.), *Developing minds* (3rd ed.). Alexandria, VA: Association for Supervision and Curriculum Development.

Cooperative Learning Center at the University of Minnesota, codirected by Johnson and Johnson. Available: http://www.clcrc.com/index.html#essays.

Corbett, H. D., & Wilson, B. L. (1991). *Testing, reform and rebellion.* Norwood, NJ: Ablex Publishing Corporation.

Curio, F. R., & Schwartz, S. L. (1998, September). There are no algorithms for teaching algorithms. *Teaching Children Mathematics, 5*(1), 26.

Davis, G. E., & Tall, D. O. (2002). What is a scheme? In D. O. Tall (Ed.), *Intelligence, learning and understanding in mathematics* (pp. 133–137). Flaxton, Australia: Post Press.

Davis, R. B. (1984). *Learning mathematics: The cognitive science approach to mathematics education.* Norwood, NJ: Albex.

DeBono, E. (1985). *Six thinking hats.* New York: Little, Brown and Company.

De Lisi, R., & Golbeck, S. (1999). The implications of Piagetian theory for peer learning. In A. M. O'Donnell & A. King (Eds.), *Cognitive perspectives on peer learning* (pp. 3–37). Mahwah, NJ: Lawrence Erlbaum Associates.

Derry, S. J., Levin, J. R., Osana, H. P., & Jones, M. S. (1998). Developing middle school students' statistical reasoning through simulation gaming. In S. J. Lajoie (Ed.), *Reflections on statistics: Agendas for learning, teaching, and assessment in K–12.* Mahwah, NJ: Lawrence Erlbaum Associates.

Dewey, J. (1933). *How we think.* Chicago: Henry Regnery.

Dienes, Z. P. (1960). *Building up mathematics.* London: Hutchinson.

Dillon, J. T. (1988). The remedial status of student questioning. *Journal of Curriculum, 20*(3), 197–210.

Echevarria, J., & Graves, A. (1998). *Sheltered content instruction: Teaching English-language learners with diverse abilities* (p. 35). Boston: Allyn and Bacon.

Ellis, A. K. (Ed.) (2001). *Research on educational innovations* (p. 105). New York: Eye on Education, Inc.

Ellis, K. A. (2001). *Research on educational innovations* (3rd ed., pp. 86–91). New York: Eye on Education, Inc..

England, D. A., & Flatley, J. K. (1985). *Homework—and why* (PDK Fastback No. 218). Bloomington, IN: Phi Delta Kappa Educational Foundation.

Feuerstein, R. (1980). *Instrumental enrichment: Intervention program for cognitive modifiability.* Baltimore, MD: University Park Press.

Feuerstein, R., Rand, Y., Hoffman, M. B., & Miller, R. (1994). In M. Ben-Hur (Ed.), *Feuerstein's instrumental enrichment.* Arlington Heights, IL: SkyLight.

Feuerstein, R., Feuerstein R., & Schur, Y. (1997). Process and content in education, particularly for retarded performers. In A. Costa & R. Liberman (Eds.), *Supporting the spirit of learning: When process is content.* Thousand Oaks, CA: Corwin Press.

Feuerstein, R., & Rand, Y. (1997). *Don't accept me as I am* (Rev. ed., pp. 337–339). Arlington Heights, IL: SkyLight.

Fischbein, E., Deri, M., Nello, M. S., & Marino, M. S. (1985). The role of implicit models in solving problems in multiplication and division. *Journal of Research in Mathematics Education, 16*(1), 3–17.

Fullan, M. (2000). The return of large-scale reform. *Journal of Educational Change, 1*(1), 1–23.

Fuson, K. C., & Kwon, Y. (1992). Korean children's understanding of multidigit addition and subtraction. *Child Development, 63*(2), 491–506.

Gange, R. M. (1985). *The conditions of learning and theory of instruction* (4th ed.). New York: Holt, Rinehart and Winston.

Geary, D. C. (1994). *Children's mathematical development: Research and practical implications.* Washington, DC: American Psychological Association.

Gelman, R. (2000). The epigenesis of mathematical thinking. *Journal of Applied Developmental Psychology, 21*(1), 27–37.

Gleitman, L., Carey, S., Newport, E., & Spelke, E. (1989). *Learning, development, and conceptual change.* A Bradford Book. Cambridge, MA: MIT Press.

Good, T. L., & Brophy, J. E. (2000). *Looking in classrooms* (8th ed.). New York: Longman.

Good, T. L., & Grouws, D. A. (1979). Teaching and mathematics learning. *Educational Leadership, 37*(1), 39–45.

Grasser, C. A., & McMahen, C. L. (1993). Anomalous information triggers questions when adults solve quantitative problems and comprehend stories. *Journal of Educational Psychology, 5*(1), 130–151.

Grasser, C. A., & Person, N. K. (1994). Question asking during tutoring. *American Education Research Journal, 31*(1), 104–137.

Haapasalo, L., & Kadijevich, D. (2000). Two types of mathematical knowledge and their relation. *Journal fur Mathematikdidatik, 21*(2), 139–157.

Harris, J. R. (1998). *The nature of assumption: Why children turn out the way they do?* New York: The Free Press and Simon & Schuster.

Hert, K. M. (1981). *Children's understanding of mathematics* (pp. 11–16). London: John Murray.

Hewson, P. W., & Hewson, M. G. (1989). Analysis and use of a task for identifying conceptions of teaching science. *Journal of Education for Teaching, 15*(3), 191–209.

Hewson, P.W., & Thorley, N. R. (1989). The conditions of conceptual change in the classroom. *International Journal of Science Education, 11*(5), 541–553.

Hiebert, J., & Carpenter, T. P. (1992). Learning and teaching with understanding. In D. Grouws (Ed.), *Handbook on research in mathematics teaching and learning*. New York: Macmillan.

Hiebert, J., & Wearne, D. (1986). Procedures over concepts: The acquisition of decimal number knowledge. In J. Hiebert (Ed.), *Conceptual and procedural knowledge: The case of mathematics* (pp. 199–223). Hillsdale, NJ: Erlbaum.

Jaworski, B. (1994). *Investigating mathematics teaching: A constructivist enquiry*. London: Falmer.

Jungck, J. R., & Calley, J .N. (1985). Strategic simulations and post-Socratic pedagogy: Constructing software to develop long term inference through experimental inquiry. *American Biology Teacher, 47*(1), 11–15.

Kahneman, D., Slovic, P., & Tversky, A. (1982). *Judgment under uncertainty: Heuristics and biases*. New York: Cambridge University Press.

Kerman, S., & Martin, M. (1980). *Teacher expectations and student achievement: Teacher handbook*. Bloomington, IN: Phi Delta Kappa.

Kerslake, D. (1986). *Fractions: Children's strategy and errors: A report of the Strategies and Errors in Secondary Mathematics Project*. Windsor, Berkshire, England: NFER-Nelson.

Kilpatrick, J., Martin, W. B., & Schifter, D. E. (Eds.). (2003). *A research companion to principals and standards for school mathematics* (p. 225). Reston, VA: National Council of Teachers of Mathematics.

Kilpatrick, J., Swafford, J., & Bradford, F. (2001). *Adding it up: Helping children learn mathematics*. Washington, DC: Center for Education, Division of Behavioral and Social Sciences and Education, National Research Council, and National Academy Press.

Koedinger, K. R., & Nathan, M. J. (1994). The real story behind story problems: Effects of representations on quantitative reasoning. *The Journal of the Learning Sciences, 12*(2). Available: http://www.shodor.org/interactivate/lessons/.

Konold, C. (1989). Informal concepts of probability. *Cognition and Instruction, 6*(1), 59–98.

Konold, C. (1991). Understanding students' beliefs about probability. In E. von Glasersfeld (Ed.), *Radical constructivism in mathematics education* (pp. 139–156). Dordrecht, The Netherlands: Reidel.

Koontz, K. L., & Berch, D. B. (1996). Identifying simple numerical stimuli: Processing inefficiencies exhibited by arithmetic learning disabled children. *Mathematical Cognition, 2*(1), 1–23.

Kozulin, A., Mangieri, J. N., & Block, C. (Eds.). (1994). *The cognitive revolution in learning in creating powerful thinking in teachers and students: Diverse perspectives*. New York: Harcourt Brace College Publishers.

Kramarski, B., & Mevarech, Z. R. (1997). Cognitive-metacognitive training within a problem solving based Logo environment. *British Journal of Educational Psychology, 67*(4), 425–445.

LaConte, R. T. (1981). *Homework as a learning experience: What research says to the teacher.* Washington, DC: National Education Association (ED 217 022).

Larrivee, B. (2000). Transforming teaching practice: Becoming the critically reflective teacher. *Reflective Practice, 1*(3), 293–308.

Lehman, D. R., Lempert, R. O., & Nisbett, R. E. (1988). The effects of graduate training on reasoning: Formal discipline and reasoning about everyday life. *American Psychologist, 43*(6), 431–443.

Lester, F. K., Jr., Masingila, J. O., Mau, S. T., Lambdin, D. V., dos Santon, V. M., & Raymond, A. M. (1994). Learning how to teach via problem solving (pp. 152–166). In D. Aichele & A. Coxford (Eds.), *Professional Development for Teachers of Mathematics.* Reston, VA: National Council of Teachers of Mathematics.

Lindsay, C. H., Greathouse, S., & Nye, B. (1988). Relationships among attitudes about homework, amount of homework assigned and completed, and student achievement. *Journal of Educational Psychology, 90*(1), 154.

Lipman, M. (1984). The cultivation of reasoning through philosophy. *Educational Leadership, 42*(1), 51–56.

Lipton, J. S., & Spelke, E. S. (2003). Origins of number sense: Large numbers discrimination in human infants. *Psychological Science, 4*(5), 396–401.

Lochhead, J., & Zietsman, A. (2001). What is problem-solving? In A. Costa (Ed.), *Developing minds* (3rd ed.). Alexandria, VA: Association for Supervision and Curriculum Development.

Long, M., & Ben-Hur, M. (1991). Informing learning through the clinical interview. *Arithmetic Teacher,* February, 44–47.

Marzano, R. J., Pickering, D. J., & Pollak, J. E. (2005). *Classroom instruction that works: Research-based strategies for increasing student achievement.* Upper Saddle River, NJ: Merrill Prentice-Hall.

Mason, J. (1993). Assessing what sense pupils make of mathematics. In M. Selinger (Ed.), *Teaching mathematics* (pp. 153–166). London: Routledge.

A Math Forum Project Elementary Problem of the Week: April 19, 1999. Good Fences—posted April 26, 1999. Available: http://mathforum.org/ elempow/solutions/ solution.ehtml?puzzle=32.

Mayer, R. (2000). Intelligence and education. In R. Sternberg (Ed.), *Handbook of intelligence* (pp. 519–533). Cambridge, MA: Cambridge University Press.

Mayer, R. E., & Wittrock, M. C. (1996). Problem solving transfer. In D. C. Berliner & R. C. Calfee (Eds.), *Handbook of educational psychology* (pp. 47–62). New York: Macmillan.

Mevarech, Z. R., & Susak, Z. (1993, March/April). Effects of learning with cooperative-mastery learning method on elementary students. *Journal of Educational Research, 86,* 197–205.

Miller, A. (1996). *Insights of genius: Imagery and creativity in science and art.* New York: Springer-Verlag.

Minsky, M. L. (1975). A framework for representing knowledge. In O. H. Winston (Ed.), *The psychology of computer vision* (pp. 211–277). New York: McGraw-Hill.

Morris, A. (1999). Developing concepts of mathematical structure: Pre-arithmetic reasoning vs. extended arithmetic reasoning. *Focus on Learning Problems in Mathematics, 21*(1), 44–71.

Nathan, M. J., & Koedinger, K. R. (2000). An investigation of teachers' beliefs of students' algebraic development. *Cognition and Instruction, 18*(2), 209–237.

National Commission on Mathematics and Science Teaching for the 21st Century (The Glenn Commission). Press Release. Sept. 27, 2000.

National Council of Teachers of Mathematics (NCTM). (1989). *Professional standards for teachers of mathematics*. Reston, VA: Author.

Nesher, P. (1986). Are mathematical understanding and algorithmic performance related? *Learning of Mathematics, 6*(3), 2–9.

Nesher, P., & Hershkovitz, S. (1994). The role of schemes in two-step problems: Analysis and research finding. *Educational Studies in Mathematics, 26*(1), 1–23.

Neuman, Y., & Schwarz, B. (2000). Substituting one mystery for another: The role of self-explanations in solving algebra word-problems. *Learning and Instruction, 10*(3), 203–220.

Nisbett, R. E., Fong, G. T., Lehman, D. R., & Cheng, P. W. (1987). Teaching reasoning. *Science, 238*(4827), 625–631.

Novak, J. D. (1977). *A theory of education*. Ithaca, NY: Cornell University Press.

Novak, J. D. (1990). Concept maps and Vee diagrams: Two metacognitive tools for science and mathematics education. *Instructional Science, 19*(1), 29–52.

Nussbaum, J. (1985). The earth as a cosmic body. In R. Diver, E. Guesne, and A. Tiberghien (Eds.), *Children's ideas in science* (pp. 170–192). Milton Keynes, UK: Open University Press.

O'Day, J. A., & Smith, M. (1993). Systemic school reform and educational opportunity. In S. Fuhrman (Ed.), *Designing coherent educational policy: Improving the system* (pp. 250–311). San Francisco: Jossey-Bass.

Palincsar, A. S., & Brown, A. L. (1984). Reciprocal teaching of comprehension fostering and comprehension monitoring activities. *Cognition and Instruction, 1*(2), 117–175.

Palincsar, A. S., & Brown, A. L. (1985). Reciprocal teaching: Activities to promote reading with your mind. In T. L. Harris & E. J. Cooper (Eds.), *Reading and concept development: Strategies for the classroom* (pp. 147–160). New York: The College Board.

Piaget, J. (1995a). From science of education and the psychology of the child. In H. E. Gruber & J. J. Vonéche (Eds.), *The essential Piaget: An interpretative reference and guide* (pp. 703–705). Northvale, NJ, and London: Jason Aronson.

Piaget, J. (1995b). Judgment and reasoning in the child (originally published in 1924). In H. E. Gruber & J. J. Vonéche (Eds.), *The essential Piaget: An interpretive reference and guide* (p. 96). Northvale, NJ: Jason Aronson.

Pilkethy, A., & Hurting, R. (1996). A review of recent research in the area of Initial Fraction Concepts. *Educational Studies in Mathematics, 30*(1) 5–36.

Plato, Translation (1892). Meno. In B. Jowett (Trans.), *The Dialogues of Plato*, (3rd ed.). London: Oxford University Press.

Pólya, G. (1945). *How to solve it: A new aspect of mathematical method.* Princeton, NJ: Princeton University Press.

Pólya, G. (1973). *How to solve it.* Princeton, NJ: Princeton University Press. (Originally copyrighted in 1945.)

Resnick, L. B., Nesher, P., Leonard, F., Magone, M., Omanson, S., & Peled, I. (1989). Conceptual bases of arithmetic errors: The case of decimal fractions. *Journal of Research in Mathematics Education, 20*(1), 8–27.

Rosenshine, B., & Meister, C. C. (1994). Reciprocal teaching: A review of the research. *Review of Educational Research, 6*(4), 479–530.

Rowe, M. B. (1996). Science, silence, and sanctions. *Science and Children, 34*(1), 35–37.

Rowland, S., Graham, E., & Berry, J. (2001). An objectivist critique of relativism in mathematics education. *Science & Education, 10*(3), 215–241.

Schmidt, W. H., McKnight, C. C., & Raizen, S. A. (1997). *A splintered vision: An investigation of U.S. science and mathematics education*. Dordrecht, The Netherlands: Kluwer.

Schoenfeld, A. H. (1987). What's all the fuss about metacognition? In A. H. Schoenfeld (Ed.), *Cognitive science and mathematics education* (pp. 190–191). Hillsdale, NJ: Lawrence Erlbaum Associates.

Schoenfeld, A. H. (1988). When good teaching leads to bad results: The disasters of "well taught" mathematics classes. *Educational Psychologist, 23*(2), 145–166.

Schoenfeld, A. H. (1992). Learning to think mathematically: Problem solving, metacognition, and sense making mathematics. In D. Grouws (Ed.), *Handbook of research on mathematics teaching and learning* (pp. 334–370). New York: Macmillan.

Schoenfeld, A. H. (Ed.). (1994). *Mathematical thinking and problem solving* (p. 60). Hillsdale, NJ: Lawrence Erlbaum Associates.

Schoenfeld, A. H. (2002, January/February). Making mathematics work for all children: Issues of standards, testing, and equity. *Educational Researcher, 31*(1), 13–25.

Schoenfeld, A. H., & Herrmann, D. (1982). Problem perception and knowledge structure in expert and novice mathematical problem solvers. *Journal of Experimental Psychology: Learning, Memory and Cognition, 8*(5), 484–494.

Scholz, R. W. (1991). Psychological research in probabilistic understanding. In R. Kapadia & M. Borovcnik (Eds.), *Chance encounters: Probability in education* (pp. 213–249). Dordrecht, The Netherlands: Kluwer Academic Publishers.

Schön, D. (1983). *The reflective practitioner.* New York: Basic Books

Sfard, A., & Linchevski, L. (1994). The gains and the pitfalls of reification: The case of algebra, *Educational Studies in Mathematics, 26*(3), 191–228.

Sfard, A. (1992). Operational origins of mathematical objects and the quandary of reification: The case of function. In G. Harel & E. Dubinsky (Eds.), *The concept of function: Aspects of epistemology and pedagogy* (pp. 59–84). MAA Notes 25. Washington: Mathematical Association of America.

Shaughnessy, J. M. (1993). Probability and statistics. *The Mathematics Teacher, 86*(3), 244–248.

Shaughnessy, J. M., & Zawojewski, J. S. (1999). Secondary students' performance on data and chance in the 1996 NAEP. *Mathematics Teacher, 92*(8), 713–718.

Shepard, L. A., & Smith, M. L. (1988). Escalating academic demand in kindergarten: Counterproductive policies. *Elementary School Journal, 89*(2), 135–145.

Shepard, R. S. (1993). Writing for conceptual development in mathematics. *Journal of Mathematical Behavior, 12*(3), 287–293.

Siegler, R. S. (2003). Implications of cognitive science research for mathematics education. In J. Kilpatrick, W. B. Martin, & D. E. Schifter (Eds.), *A research companion to principles and standards for school mathematics* (p. 225). Reston, VA: National Council of Teachers of Mathematics.

Silver, E. A. (1979). Student perceptions of relatedness among mathematical verbal problems. *Journal for Research in Mathematics Education, 10*(3), 195–210.

Silver, E. A. (1994). On mathematical problem posing. *For the Learning of Mathematics, 14*(1), 19–28.

Silver, E. A., Alacaci, C., & Stylianou, D. A. (2000). Students' performance on extended constructed-response tasks. In E. A. Silver & P. A. Kenny (Eds.) *Results from the seventh mathematics assessment of the National Assessment of Educational Progress* (pp. 301–341). Reston, VA: National Council of Teachers of Mathematics.

Silver, E. A., & Cai, J. (1993). *Mathematical problem posing by middle school students.* Paper presented at the annual meeting of the American Educational Research Association, Atlanta, GA.

Skemp, R. R. (1962). The need for schematic learning theory. *British Journal of Educational Psychology, 32*(2), 133–142.

Skemp, R. R. (1976). Relational understanding and instrumental understanding. *Mathematics Teaching, 77*(1), 20–26.

Skemp, R. R. (1986). *The psychology of learning mathematics* (2nd ed.). Middlesex, England: Plenum.

Smith, M. U. (1991). A view from biology. In M. U. Smith (Ed.), *Toward a unified theory of problem solving* (pp. 1–20). Hillsdale, NJ: Lawrence Erlbaum.

Smith, M., & Cohen, M. (1991, September). A national curriculum in the United States? *Educational Leadership, 49*(1), 74–81.

Spinelli, C. G. (2001). Interactive teaching strategies and authentic curriculum and assessment: A model for effective classroom instruction. *Hong Kong Special Education Forum, 4*(1), 3–12.

Staver, J. R. (1998). Constructivism: Sound theory for explicating the practice of science and science teaching. *Journal of Research in Science Teaching, 35*(5), 501–520.

Stein, D. (2004). *Teaching critical reflection.* Washington, DC: Office of Educational Research and Improvement, U.S. Department of Education. Available: http://ericacve.org .

Suchting, W. A. (1986). *Marx and philosophy: Three studies.* Hampshire, UK: Macmillan Press Ltd.

Tall, D. (2002). Continuities and discontinuities in long-term learning schemas. In D. Tall & M. Thomas (Eds.), *Intelligence, learning and understanding in mathematics: A tribute to Richard Skemp* (pp. 151–178). Flaxton, Australia: Post Press.

Thorley, N. R. (1990, August). *The role of conceptual change model in the interpretation of classroom interactions.* Unpublished doctoral dissertation, University of Wisconsin, Madison.

University of Chicago School Math Project: Transition Mathematics. (1998). *Scott Foresman integrated mathematics* (2nd ed.). Glenview, IL: Scott Foresman.

Van Hiele, P. (1986). *Structure and insight. A theory of mathematics education.* Orlando, FL: Academic Press Inc.

Von Glasersfeld, E. (1995). *Radical constructivism: A way of knowing and learning.* London: Falmer.

Von Glasersfeld, E. (1996). Introduction: Aspects of constructivism. In C. T. Fosnot (Ed.), *Constructivism: Theory, perspectives, and practice.* New York: Teachers College Press.

Von Glasersfeld, E. (1998). Why constructivism must be radical. In M. Larochelle, N. Bednarz, & J. Garrison (Eds.), *Constructivism and education* (pp. 23–28). Cambridge, UK: Cambridge University Press.

Vygotsky, L. (1978). *Mind in society.* Cambridge, MA: Harvard University Press.

Vygotsky, L. S. (1986). *Thought and language* (A. Kozulin, Trans. and Ed.). Cambridge, MA: MIT Press.

Walberg, H. J., Paschal, R. A., & Weinstein, T. (1985, April). Homework's powerful effects on learning. *Educational Leadership, 42*(7), 76–79.

Watanabe, T. (2002). Learning from Japanese lesson study. *Educational Leadership, 59*(6), 36–39.

Wiggins, G. (1990). The case for authentic assessment. *Practical Assessment, Research & Evaluation, 2*(2). Available: http://ericae.net/pre/getvn.asp?v=2&n=2.

Wilson, L. D., & Blank, R. K. (1999). *Improving mathematics education using results from NAEP and TIMMS.* Washington, DC: Council of Chief State School Officers. Available: http://publications.ccsso.org/ccsso/publications_detail.cfm?PID=212. [July 10, 2001].

Index

Page numbers appearing in italics refer to figures.

A

algebra
  mental representation and, 59, 61–62
  overgeneralization of algebraic forms, 49
  preconceptions in school arithmetic, algebra, geometry, and probability and statistics, *45*
  solution of consequential subproblems, 101
  transition from arithmetical to algebraic thinking, 46–47
  typical categories of classification for algebraic word problems, by context, 89
  word problem solving and, 72–73, 96–97
analogies
  by context, 88–89, *89*
  by functional schemata, 89–92
analysis questions, 26, *26*
Anderson, John
  dual-knowledge system and, 9
Annenberg Institute for School Reform
  homework analysis, 116
Archimedes series computer programs for problem solving, 94–95
arithmetic
  fourth grade students' ability to retell story problems, 96
  illustrating word problems, 97
  imagery and, 80
  mental representation and, 59
  mental representations and, 61–62
  preconceptions in school arithmetic, algebra, geometry, and probability and statistics, *45*
  transition from arithmetical to algebraic thinking, 46–47
Assessment Standards for School Mathematics
  portfolios and, 124
assessments
  criterion-referenced and norm-referenced, 109
  formative, 111–128
  homework analysis, 115–117, 128
  individual interviews around problem-solving activities, 117–121, 128
  inferences about students' reasoning and learning and, 110, 127
  journal writing, 121–122, 128
  organizing and integrating data from, 128
  performance-based, 126–127
  portfolios, 124–126, 128
  process-oriented compared with product-oriented alternative assessments, 110–111, vii
  self-monitoring, 122–123, 128
  summative, 111, 127
authentic assessment practices, 111

B

Bloom, Benjamin
  Taxonomy of Educational Objectives, 11
Brown, A. L.
  reciprocal instruction and, 65–66
Bruner, J.
  stages in concept development, 11–12
bugs. *See* systematic errors

C

centrality characteristic of structural cognitive change, 5
classroom communication and observations
  collecting observation information, 113–115
  forms and purpose of, 112
  sharing observations with students, 115
  surveys and, 115
  teacher as participant-observer, 113, 128
  teacher's checklist for cognitive behaviors of word problem solving in geometry, *113–114*
  timing of observations, 115
classroom culture
  classroom communication and observations and, 112
  solving problems mathematically and, 85, 94
Coalition for Better Schools
  homework analysis, 116
communication. *See also* classroom communication and observations
  altering misconceptions and, 66–68
  appropriate communication, *67*
  asking questions of the teacher, 94
  formal verbal language of mathematics and, 66–68
  interviews and, 119
  reasons for failure of, 66
  solving problems mathematically and, 91–92
computer programs
  problem-solving series, 94–95
  simulation of systematic errors and, 44
concept maps
  meta-knowledge and, 64–65, *65*

Concept-Rich Instruction
  basis for, 11, 55–56, 129
  decontextualization, 12, 18–31, vi
  description, 69, 129–130
  description of teacher activity, *131–133*
  five components of, 12–40, *13,* 129–130
  formal school assessment and typical
    quizzes and, 110
  formative assessment and, 111–127, 130
  major mathematical concepts for
    grades 6-8, *135–136*
  meaning: encapsulating a generalization
    in words, 12, 32–35
  practice, 12, 13–17
  realization, 12, 39–40
  recontextualization, 12, 36–39
  reflection and, 11, 12, vi
  teacher role, 15–16, 27, 28–31, 33–35,
    36–39, 40–41, 129–130, *131–133,* v–viii
conceptual-change view, 6–7
conceptual knowledge
  "bottom-up" and "top-down" knowledge
    development, 3, 6, 10
  conceptual changes and, 4, 6–7
  constructivism, 3–10, 129
  debates over epistemology, 1–2
  declarative knowledge *versus* procedur-
    al knowledge, *7*
  direct learning compared with mediat-
    ed learning, 9, 10
  distinction between human conscious-
    ness and it objects, and between sci-
    entific truth and common sense, 2
  "dual-knowledge system," 8–9
  "dynamic action" practice, 8
  empiricist view, 7
  fractions case example, 2–3
  instructional practices, 7–9
  major mathematical concepts for
    grades 6-8, *135–136*
  procedural knowledge and, 6–9
  relationship between conceptual knowl-
    edge and procedural knowledge: from
    theory to instructional practice, *7*
  "simultaneous action" practice, 8
  structural cognitive changes, 4–5, 10
constructivism
  cognitive structure and, 4–5, 129, v
  conceptual changes and, 4
  debate over the nature of the process
    of knowing, 3–10
  misconceptions and, 43
  shift of research from content to mental
    predicates, language, and precon-
    cepts, 4, 129
  strategies for effectively teaching how
    to solve problems mathematically,
    73–74
  understanding as an active process, 3
contextual analogies, 88–89, *89*
cooperative learning. *See also* Reciprocal
  instruction
  altering misconceptions and, 68–69
  conditions for effectiveness, 68–69

  Ms. Smith's example of a modified les-
    son on polynomials and, 58–59
  recontextualization and, 38–39
  students' social judgment and, 68
count all strategy, 5, 8
count on strategy, 5, 8
counterintuitive concepts
  intuition role in mathematics, 50
  non-Euclidian geometry and, 51
  probability and statistics, 52
  typical counterintuitive notions in prob-
    ability and statistics, *53*
criterion-referenced assessment
  disadvantages of, 109

D
David, R. B.
  structural cognitive change and, 4
DeBono, E.
  mediation of meta-cognitive awareness
    model, 63–64
declarative knowledge. *See* conceptual
  knowledge
decontextualization
  description, 12, 18
  encouragement of divergent responses,
    27
  higher-order questioning and, 19, 20–27
  practice and, 18–19
  reflection and, 18, 19, 28–31
  skills drills and, 18
  student reflection over errors, 28–31
  three representations of 1 3/4 : 1/2, *19*
  wait time and, 19, 27
Dewey, John
  adaptation as the function of human
    intelligence, 1
  reviewing the solution to check the
    result and, 105–106
direct instruction
  mediated learning and, 9, 10
  practice and, 13
discovery learning, 33
drills
  practice component of Concept-Rich
    Instruction, 13, 15–16
dual-knowledge system
  description, 8–9
dynamic action practice
  description, 8
dynamic assessment practices, 111

E
EADIM. *See* Error Analysis Diagnosis in
  Mathematics
empiricist view, 7
english proficiency
  classroom discussions and, 112
  key words and non-native English
    speakers, 86
epistemology
  debates over, 1–2
  value of, 3
Error Analysis Diagnosis in Mathematics,
  44

errors. *See also* misconceptions; trial and error strategy
  as instructional tools, 28, 52–55, vi
  organization of students' responses on the board, *30*
  perception of as unfortunate mistakes, 54
  sixth grade classroom discussion example, 29–31, *30,* 33–34
  student reflection over errors, 28–31
Euclid's five postulates, *51*

F

Feuerstein, Reuven
  cognitive function classification, 81, *82,* 115
  Instrumental Enrichment research, 63–64
  mediated learning experience and, 55–56
flexibility
  altering misconceptions and, 56–59, 130
  decimal fractions example, 57–58
  Ms. Smith's example of a modified lesson on polynomials, 58–59
  teacher flexibility during interviews, 120
formative assessments
  authentic and dynamic practices and, 111
  benefits of, 128, 130
  classroom communication and observations, 112–115
  combining with summative assessment, 128
  compared with summative assessments, 111, 127
  description, 111, 127
  homework analysis, 115–117
  individual interviews around problem-solving activities, 117–121
  journal writing, 121–122
  learning to perform, 127–128
  organizing and integrating data from, 128
  performance-based, 126–127
  portfolios, 124–126
  self-monitoring, 122–123
  tasks and rubrics for, 111
  testing new teaching strategies and, 127
fractions
  decimal fractions example of flexibility, 57–58
  the factor and product model of division, *61*
  the measurement model of division, *60*
  overgeneralization and the addition and subtraction of, 49, 50
  the partitive model of division, *60*
functional analogies, 89–92

G

Gange, Robert
  hierarchy for learning mathematical concepts, 11

geometry
  application of problem-based instruction to the geometrical concepts of perimeter and area, 76–77
  Euclid's five postulates, *51*
  imagery and, 80, 97
  mental representation and, 59
  misconceptions in geometry, *29*
  non-Euclidian, 51
  plane geometry portfolio example, 124
  Plato's *Meno* example, 20–26
  Schoenfeld's problem-solving comparison of students and mathematicians, 104–105
  teacher's checklist for cognitive behaviors of word problem solving in geometry, *113–114*
  verbal terms and, 87
Glenn Commission
  position on the current state of mathematics education, 40
graphic organizers
  concept maps, 64–65
  meta-knowledge and, 64–65
group work. *See* Cooperative learning

H

Harvard Project Zero
  homework analysis, 116
Hegel, G. W. F.
  knowledge definition, 1
higher-order questioning
  analysis questions, 26, *26*
  decontextualization and, 20–27, *21*
  inference questions, 26, *26*
homework
  benefits of, 115
  effective homework practices, 116
  goals of, 115
  practice component of Concept-Rich Instruction and, 13–14, 15
  problem-solving notebook entries, 116–117
  student achievement level and, 115
  students who cannot complete or incorrectly complete homework and, 117
Hunter, Madeline
  Instructional Theory Into Practice, 16

I

imagery. *See* mental representation
inference questions, 26, *26*
Instructional Theory Into Practice teaching model, 16
Instrumental Enrichment, 63–64
interviews
  clinical interviews as a model for an alternative assessment strategy, 117
  concluding, 120–121
  effective design for, 118
  goals for, 119
  individual, 118, 119–121, 128
  interruptions and, 120
  open-ended questions and, 120, 128
  place value example, 118
  of selected students, 118

set-up for, 119–120
small groups and, 118–119
teacher flexibility and, 120
three stages of, 117–118
intuition. *See* counterintuitive concepts

J
journal writing
analysis of, 122
benefits of, 121
entries for, 121, 122
language for, 122
student sharing of entries with each
other, 122

K
Kant, Immanuel
knowledge definition, 1, v
key words
non-native English speakers and, 86
solving problems mathematically and,
72, 85–87, *86*

L
language. *See also* communication
for journal writing, 122
precise use of language in problem
solving, 85–87
translating word problems into
mathematical equations, graphs, or
diagrams, 96–100
translation of verbal information on
relationships to mathematical codes,
87
Likert scale ratings
collecting observation information and,
115
Lipman, M.
mediation of meta-cognitive awareness
model, 63–64
low-performing students
"discovery learning" and, 33
Feuerstein's Instrumental Enrichment
and, 64
homework and, 13–14, 15
mental representation of algebraic symbols and, 61–62
problem-solving instruction and, 72, 75,
77–78, 81, vi–vii
wait time and, 27

M
major mathematical concepts for grades
6–8, *135–136*
Marx, Karl
truth as the product of interpretation,
1–2
Marzano, R. J.
higher-order questioning, 26, *26*
*Teacher Expectations and Student
Achievement,* 19
meaning
adding variations to the concept and, 35
assumption that meaning is transported
from a speaker to a listener and, 34
avoiding problems, 34–35
conceptualization and deep meaning, *32*

description, 12, 32
differing conceptual structure among
individual students and, 34
"discovery learning" and, 33
the evolution of children's notion of
Earth's shape, *35*
examples of middle school mathematical concepts, *35*
hierarchy of concepts and, 32
independent learning and, 32
mindless practice and, 32
problems in the construction of new
concepts, 34–35
sixth grade classroom discussion example, 33–34
"telling" about concepts and, 33
mediated learning experience
direct learning and, 9, 10
Feuerstein's views, 55–56
reciprocal relationship between
teachers and learners and, 55–56
reflection and, 11
Meno (Plato), 20–26
mental representation
altering misconceptions and, 59–62
the factor and product model of division, *61*
internal and external representations,
61–62, 97–99
the measurement model of division, *60*
the partitive model of division, *60*
solving problems mathematically and,
79–80
meta-cognitive awareness
altering misconceptions and, 62–66
goal of, 63
graphic organizers and, 64–65
meta-cognition, *103*
reciprocal instruction and, 65–66
Reflection-in-Action instructional
strategy, 62–63
solving problems mathematically and,
100, 101, *103,* 103–105
Mind Bugs computer program, 44
Minsky, M. L.
structural cognitive change and, 4
misconceptions
alternative mental representations,
59–62, 70
appropriate communication, 66–68, 70
basis for, 43
challenge of altering, 42
constructive interaction among learners, 68–69, 70
counterintuitive concepts, 50–52, *53*
errors as instructional tools, 52–55, vi
an example of students' false perception of mathematical knowledge, *28*
flexibility and, 56–59, 70, 130
informed teachers' efforts, 42–43
mega-cognitive awareness, 62–66, 70
misconceptions in geometry, *29*
objective logic and psycho-logic and,
43, 70
overgeneralizations, 47–50, 70

pace of instruction and, vi
preconceptions, 43, 44–45, *45*
reciprocity and, 56, *57,* 70, 130
rectangle example, 43–44
resistance to change, 54–55
right angle example, 43
six instructional principles for conceptual remediation, 55–69, 70
students' typical misconceptions about
solving problems mathematically, 74
systematic errors, 44
undergeneralizations, 46–47, 70
uninformed teachers' efforts, 43
of zero as nothing, 44
MLE. *See* mediated learning experience

N

national achievement tests
summative assessment example, 111
National Council of Teachers of
Mathematics
knowledge standards, 6, 52, 74, 107,
119, 130, v
vision of school mathematics, vii
No Child Left Behind Act
problem-based instruction and, 75
norm-referenced assessment
disadvantages of, 109

O

observations. *See* classroom
communication and observations
open-ended questions
interviews and, 120, 128
overgeneralizations
algebraic forms and, 49, 50
extension of the number system from
natural numbers to integers and from
whole numbers to rational numbers
and, 47–48
fractions and, 49
multidigit subtraction among third
grade students example, 48
rote learning and, 49
telling students the correct answers,
concepts, or procedures and, 50

P

Palincsar, A. S.
reciprocal instruction and, 65–66
performance-based assessment
continuous feedback and, 127
description, 126
goal of, 126
steps for, 126
value of, 126–127
permanence characteristic of structural
cognitive change, 5
pervasiveness of change
neuroplasticity of the brain and, 5
Vygotsky's views, 5
Piaget, J.
cognitive development research, 5, 32
conceptualization as a shift of operation from a plane of action to a plane
of thought, 14

model of assimilation and accommodation, 8
reflective process, 18
Plato
Meno, 20–26
Pólya, George
components of the problem solving
process, 81, *83,* 83–105, 108
reviewing the solution to check the
result and, 105–106
polynomials
Ms. Smith's example of a modified
lesson on, 58–59
portfolio assessment
benefits of, 126
plane geometry example of contents,
124
portfolio description, 124
strategies for developing, 124–125
student choice of contents, 125
types of portfolios, 125
practice
amount necessary, 14–15
decontextualization and, 18–19
description, 12, 13–14
drills and, 13
false indicators that practice has been
sufficient, 14–15
fine-tuning tasks, 16
homework and, 13–14, 15
matching the level of task difficulty
with the students' improving abilities
and, 16
meaning and, 32
nature of repetition and, 15–16
novelty and challenge and, 16–17, *17*
reflection and, 14
Zone of Proximal Development and, 14
preconceptions
overgeneralizations, 47–50
preconceptions in school arithmetic,
algebra, geometry, and probability
and statistics, *45*
prevalence in the classroom, 45
undergeneralizations, 46–47
probability and statistics
false intuition and, 52
preconceptions in school arithmetic,
algebra, geometry, and probability
and statistics, *45*
typical counterintuitive notions in probability and statistics, *53*
procedural knowledge
description, 6
process-oriented alternative assessments
compared with product-oriented
assessments, 110–111, vii
portfolios and, 124
product-oriented alternative assessments
compared with process-oriented
assessments, 110–111, vii
Pythagorean theorem
Plato's *Meno* example, 20–26

R

rational numbers
    extension of the number system from
        whole numbers to rational numbers,
        47–48
    subcontexts of, 46
    undergeneralizations and, 46
realization
    description, 12, 39
    school environment and, 39–40
reciprocal instruction
    application to mathematics instruction,
        66
    meta-cognitive awareness and, 65–66
reciprocity
    altering misconceptions and, 56, 130
    between teacher and student, *57*
recontextualization
    cooperative learning and, 38–39
    description, 12, 36
    recontextualizing the concept of the
        coefficient as slope and intercept by
        comparing and contrasting, *38*
    teacher role, 37–39
    third grade classroom discussion exam-
        ple, 36–37
reflection. *See also* meta-cognitive
    awareness
    decontextualization and, 18, 19
    interviews and, 128
    journal writing and, 121, 122
    learning of mathematical concepts and,
        11–12
    mediated learning and, 11
    practice and, 14
    solving problems mathematically and,
        72, 103–104, 108
    student reflection over errors, 28–31
Reflection-in-Action instructional strategy,
    62–63
repetition
    skills drills for standardized tests,
        15–16
reviewing the solution
    importance of, 105–106
    reflections for guidance in, 107
rote learning
    conceptual understanding and, vi
    overgeneralizations and, 49
Rowe, Mary Budd
    wait time research, 27

S

Sartre, Jean Paul
    truth as the product of interpretation,
        1–2
schemata
    analogies by, 89–92
    complex schemata in solving two-step
        word problems, *91*
    order of difficulty in terms of the basic
        mathematical operations, 90
    problems by common contextual cate-
        gories analyzed by relationships and
        schemata, *92–93*
    simple and complex types, 90–91
    simple schemata in solving one-step
        word problems, *90*
schematic changes. *See* structural
    cognitive changes
Schoenfeld, Alan
    problem-solving comparison of stu-
        dents and mathematicians, 104–105
Schön, D.
    Reflection-in-Action instructional strate-
        gy, 62–63
self-monitoring
    penny stacking example, 123
    solving problems mathematically and,
        103–105
    student assessment and, 122–123, 128
    value of, 123
self-regulation
    solving problems mathematically and,
        84–85
showcase portfolios
    description, 125
Sierra computer program, 44
simultaneous action practice
    description, 8
Skemp, R. R.
    levels of conceptual understanding, 12
    structural cognitive change and, 4
Socratic questioning
    Plato's *Meno* example, 20–26, *21*
solving problems mathematically
    advantages of problem-based instruc-
        tion, 75–76
    algebra example, 72–73
    analogies by context, 88–89
    analogies by functional schemata,
        89–92
    application to geometrical concepts of
        perimeter and area, 76–77
    arguments against problem-based
        instruction, 74–75
    asking questions and, 94
    classroom culture and, 85, 94
    classroom dialogue and, 91–92
    cognitive challenges of solving word
        problems, 78–85
    conceptual development and, 108
    constructivist approach, 73–74
    as content knowledge, 71, 72
    defining the problem, 93–107
    doing exercises compared with solving
        problems, 71–72
    error analysis, 79–80, 84
    examples of implicit mathematical rela-
        tionships, 87
    expert *versus* novice problem solv-
        ing, *106*
    factors determining the difficulty of
        solving word problems, 78
    final goal of complex word problems, 96
    graphic representation of a word prob-
        lem, *98*
    hierarchy of mathematical concepts
        and, 78
    imaging strategies and, 79–80

impulsivity and, 84
instructional challenge of teaching
    word problems, 73–78
key words and, 72, 85–87, *86*
logical operational abilities and, 81
low-performing students and, 72, 75,
    77–78, 81, vi–vii
managerial functions and, 102
as a means for finding correct answers,
    71, 72
meta-cognition and follow-up cognitive
    functions, *104*
meta-cognitive awareness and, 100, 101,
    103, 103–105
planning the solution, 101–103
Pólya's components of the problem-
    solving process, 81, *83*, 83–105, 108
precise use of language and, 85–87
problem solving as instructional ends,
    77–78
the problem-solving process, *83*
as a process or ability, 71, 72
reasons for students' failure, 78
reasons for students' success, 78–79
reflection and, 72
relating a problem to past experiences,
    88–92
reviewing the solution, 105–107
self-monitoring and, 103–105
self-regulation of input, 84–85
solution of consequential subproblems,
    101–102
solving the problem, 103–105
strategic competence and, 78–79
students' typical misconceptions
    about, 74
subproblems and, 96, 101, 108
teacher's checklist for cognitive behav-
    iors of word problem solving in
    geometry, *113–114*
textbook publishers and, 72
translating word problems into mathe-
    matical equations, graphs, or dia-
    grams, 96–100
"trial and error" and, 102, 105
understanding the problem, 84
U.S. students compared with students
    from other countries and, 107–108
variations in problem definitions, *95*
wait time and, 85
working memory and, 81
state achievement tests
    summative assessment example, 111
statistics. *See* probability and statistics
structural cognitive changes
    centrality characteristic, 5
    "count all" and "count on" strategies,
        5, 8, 10
    description, 4
    permanence characteristic, 5
    pervasive nature of, 4–5
summative assessments
    combining with formative assessment,
        128

compared with formative assessment,
    111
surveys
    collecting observation information and,
        115
systematic errors
    computer programs to simulate, 44

T
Taxonomy of Educational Objectives
    (Bloom), 11
teacher alternative assessment portfolios
    description, 125
*Teacher Expectations and Student
    Achievement* (Marzano), 19
teacher-student portfolios
    description, 125
tests. *See* assessments
Third International Mathematics and
    Science Study
    problem-based instruction and, 75
TIMSS. *See* Third International
    Mathematics and Science Study
translation of word problems
    association of worded presentations
        with other representations, 98–99
    difficulties of, 96–100
    graphic representation of a word prob-
        lem, *98*
    representation as a volitional act, *99*
    setting priorities and making judg-
        ments, 100
    type of information available and, 97–98
trial and error strategy
    solving problems mathematically and,
        102, 105
trigonometry
    imagery and, 80
    relating a problem to past experiences,
        88

U
undergeneralizations
    generalizing mathematical ideas, *47*
    rational numbers example, 46
    transition from arithmetical to algebra-
        ic thinking and, 46–47

V
Venn diagrams
    meta-knowledge and, 64
Vygotsky, L. S.
    basis for Concept-Rich Instruction, 55
    pervasive nature of structural cognitive
        change, 5
    Zone of Proximal Development, 14

W
wait time
    decontextualization and, 19, 27
    solving problems mathematically and,
        85
word problems. *See* solving problems
    mathematically

Z
Zone of Proximal Development, 14

About the Author

Meir Ben-Hur is vice president, Program Services, and lead math consultant for the International Renewal Institute, Inc. (IRI). Since his first meeting with Reuven Feuerstein convinced him to devote a lifetime of learning and teaching to the Israeli psychologist's systematic approach to mediating children's learning experiences, Meir has developed his knowledge and skills as a teacher of young students and adults. His special interest in  Feuerstein's Instrumental Enrichment (FIE) has been in bridging FIE's "learning how to learn" process into mathematics.

Meir has served as a senior international trainer for Feuerstein's institutes in Brazil, Israel, Holland, and England. In addition, Meir has led the development of the International Center for the Enhancement of Learning Potential's (ICELP) trainers at the North American and international institutes, written several articles and books, including *Cognitive Pathways to Achievement in Mathematics*, led IRI's development of the Math Advantage Achievement Program, coordinated IRI's achievement research model, and directed lead teacher training programs in Cleveland, New York, St. Louis, San Francisco, Fresno, Los Angeles, Chicago, and other smaller districts. In addition to consulting with training programs in schools and industry, Meir consults with North American Authorized Training Centers and ICELP on development of adult trainers for all versions of FIE.